EROTIC FAIRY TALES

Englished from the French of the

ABBÉ DE VOISENON

NEW YORK: PRIVATELY PRINTED

For Private Collectors of Erotica

THE PANURGE PRESS

J. A. J. finx.

CONTENTS

INTRODUCTION

INTRODUCTION

Claude Henri de Fusée, Abbé de Voisenon, the author of these Erotic Fairy
Tales, led an interesting though un-
eventful life. His earthly pilgrimage
was confined to France and lasted from
1708 to 1775. This period was an un-
ruffled interlude between the gay mock-
ing days of Louis XIV and the grim
terrors of the French Revolution. Oddly
enough, although Voisenon's own life
was as devoid of dramatic vicissitudes
as the age in which he lived, his brilliant
personality and speed of wit inclined
him to dramatic writing.

We do not know too much of Voisenon because, unlike so many of his
contemporaries, he never wrote his
memoirs. Yet one or two stories about

him are of more than casual interest. At the age of ten, little Claude Henri wrote a verse letter to Voltaire. Voltaire was astonished at its precocity and asked the boy to visit him. For half a century afterwards they were friends— a none too easy task, for Voltaire was the most impatient and hot-headed of geniuses and quarreled with almost everybody. In middle age Voisenon entered the priesthood. Contemporary rumor explained that this had been brought about by a duel in which Voisenon was deliberately the aggressor and which had filled him with remorse. This apocryphal tale however does not jibe with his character at all nor did it determine any change in his manner of living.

The literature of Voisenon's age was predicated upon and centered about two objects: wit and women. This at once explains its sparkle, its naughtiness, its charm, and its droll laughter. Just as in the preceding century the Court of the roi Soleil dictated the atmosphere of French literary life—the letters of Madame de Sevigné, the tragedies of Racine, the criteria of Boileau, the comedies of Molière, the fables of La Fontaine, the maxims of La Rochefoucauld—so in the eighteenth century was French literature nurtured in the salons of illustrious and accomplished women. All the facets of wit and conversation were cultivated: epigrams, repartee, bon mots, brilliant compliments, paradoxes. And all these facets were sharpened and made more glittering by the presence of the cultivated hostesses of these literary drawing-rooms. Goethe, whose judgments

on such matters are peculiarly accurate, and who viewed this age from a
foreign vantage-point, regarded it as
one of the most interesting periods in
history.

In the midst of this intellectual word-
play and salon social life, Voisenon
played no insignificant part. His portrait fitted into the frame perfectly.
Handsome he was and gracious, and
knew how to pay compliments in the
most delicious original way. Madame
du Barry and Madame de Pompadour
and a dozen other distinguished women
were his friends. He was welcomed
everywhere and repeatedly. At the age
of twenty he had made his début as a
dramatist with a witty piece. Every
year thereafter some new witty offering
of his appeared: dramas, essays, verses,
and short stories. These were dis-

cussed and laughed over in the salons, and his presence always added gayety to the occasion. His versatility even included musical compositions: oratorios, ballets, and dozens of minor pieces.

Upon entering the priesthood, Voisenon became vicar-general to the important bishop of Boulogne. But his scintillating spirit and the glamor of past social triumphs chafed at the isolation of religious life. Thus, when the bishop died not long afterwards, Voisenon requested and received the abbey of Jard for it required neither residence nor duties. Now, as abbé, he began to write more than ever before. He constantly contributed articles on a variety of subjects to various journals of the day, interspersing these with plays of consummate verve. In 1746 Voisenon produced his masterpiece, Coquette

Fixée, a tremendous hit, and all Paris was abuzz with its epigrams.

By modern standards the priest-playwright would seem altogether incongruous and paradoxical. But eighteenth century France accepted such a phenomenon as natural if not usual. Voisenon's priestly vestments added the unexpected to his repartee, pique to his wit, and color to his gracious compliments. More and more was he sought after in the most distinguished literary circles. In 1762 he was elected to the French Academy. This honor gratified him profoundly for since his ordination he had sought to impart in his writings, beneath the veneer of sophisticated sparkle, veiled comments on life, moral precepts which the solitude of his vicarage days had taught him.

The last few years of Voisenon's life

were touched by the wounds of ingratitude and disfavor. The brilliant fabric of French society was already becoming singed by the heat of imminent revolution. In a number of articles he defended some friends who sought to abolish the parlement. These articles lost him many influential friends, and the entrée to a number of prominent salons. He retired to his château at Voisenon and died shortly afterwards.

The two erotic fairy tales which comprise this volume have never before been published in the United States though they are representative of Voisenon's wittiest and most polished work. His age was saturate with romantic imagination and many of his fellowmen of letters employed the fairy tale as the most elastic medium of expression. But

they must not be compared nor confused with nursery tales.

The origin and development of fairy
tales is not so naive, whimsical and
dreamy as one might guess off-hand.
They are essentially folk-tales and go
back to the immemorial Indic Vedas, to
prehistoric Egyptian nature-myths, and
to the taboos and totemism of savage society the world over. This belief in
fairies forms part of the superstitions of
almost all primitive peoples and belongs
no less to the childhood of humanity
than to the reader's personal childhood.

The curious fact is that actual fairies
seldom people our most famous fairy
tales, such as those of Hans Christian
Andersen or the brothers Grimm. As
long as there is some supernatural ele-
ment in a tale, we regard it as of that
type. The tales of Voisenon which are

here included contain fairies, rollicking, frolicking fairies of a genus altogether apart from those which delighted our immaturity. Behind their obvious, if unspoken, commentaries on the foibles of men and women, lies the passage of countless centuries. For the fairy tale is in its own unique way a true index of time and progress and the growth of civilization. From the Arabian Nights to Shakespeare's Midsummer Night's Dream, from the Odyssey of Homer to Alice in Wonderland, from the Golden Ass of Apuleius to Voisenon can be measured the transit of man's intellectual development.

We Americans, among the nations of the world the youngest born, have already contributed generously to the domain of the fairy tale. Joel Chandler Harris, with his imperishable creations of Brer Rabbit and Brer Fox, stands with the greatest of folk-lorists. And the Paul Bunyan myths, still in the process of formation, are even of deeper significance than Baron Munchausen. Of the lesser contributions, perhaps the most notable American erotic fairy tale —for it is that and nothing else— is Cabell's Jurgen, which can favorably compare in influence with the whimsical and juvenile legacy of James Barrie.

Voisenon's Royal Bed of Roses and Rhapsody Risque are fairy tales written for adults only. They are brittle, scintillating pieces spiced in the most sophisticated manner of eighteenth century France. And how modern and up-to-date they are in their subtlety and the eternal battle of the sexes! Obvious too that Voisenon knew women, the candle ever ready for the flame, with the in-gredients of flesh and spirit, perfume and powder, properly proportioned. And his fairies! Were there ever such human and mischievous elves anywhere outside of Voisenon's pages? They are tireless in their pranks, always up to some new fantastic trick and the reader never knows what they will do on the next page. If they are too often risque and naughty, the intelligent reader willingly enough forgives them—or shall we say, thanks them? It is indeed a pity that we grown-ups have so few fairy tales of such magic.

And if we surrender ourselves completely to the gayety of Voisenon's stories, there is yet further profit for us. Voisenon's nimble wit is sprinkled with quick observations snatched from life and moral precepts which our author does not allow to interfere with the run-

ning action. These tales mirror the life
of his age with superb sufficiency for
they reflect and refract at once the lights
and shadows of his contemporaries. No
wonder Voltaire enjoyed their pervad-
ing buoyancy of style. No wonder too
that Octave Uzanne could say: "With
the exception of Voltaire, Voisenon per-
sonified the sympathetic spirit of his age
better than any other writer."

Herman Mars

ROYAL BED OF ROSES

ROYAL BED OF ROSES

Chapter I

Which Promises More than it Contains

Prince Potiron was uglier than his name implies; Prince Tactful was charming; Princess Tricolore was fresher & brighter than a Spring morning: she loathed Potiron, adored Tactful, and was forced to marry Potiron. All the better for her!

To tell a story like that would be inartistic. You get the conclusion at the same time as the plot; but you do not understand why it is all for the best, and that is what I am going to unravel with all the pomp suitable to the gravity of the subject.

Potiron, although ugly, stupid and un-
gainly, was not legitimate. His mother
was so unattractive that no man had
been brave enough to marry her; but
her wealth stood her in the stead of
charms; she bought her lovers, and the
only sums she ever did were in the cal-
culation of her pleasure: she paid for it
according to the time it lasted. She always paid in installments, and Potiron
had been manufactured by piece-work.

He had a gigantic head with nothing
at all inside it; his legs were as stunted
as his ideas; so that when he was either
walking or thinking, he never arrived
anywhere; but, as he had heard it said
that intelligent men do foolish things
but never say them, he tried to make a
show of intelligence by getting married.

His mother, the Fairy Rancor, reflected a long time before deciding upon

which family she would inflict this scourge, and her choice finally came to rest on Princess Tricolore, daughter of the Queen of the Patagonians. This Queen despised her husband and took no interest in her children, and she made a great to-do about love, though very little of her lovers; she was ruled more by sensations than by sentiments: a very lucky disposition to possess. A year after her marriage she gave birth to a Prince who showed signs of great promise. Soon a great argument took place amongst the Council on the question of his education. The King claimed that, as a foreigner, he had a right to place his son in the College of the Four Nations. The Queen objected to this; the King insisted; the Queen held her ground; the discussion became more and more embittered, and the little

Prince, who, apparently, had charming qualities, ended the quarrel by dying.

The Queen, who wanted to continue the argument, determined to have another boy: she told all her friends of her intention; she was delighted when she became pregnant, but all she gave birth to was a daughter: which distressed her terribly. The question of a name for this little Princess was very carefully considered. At that time the Queen had only three lovers, of whom the first was fair, the second dark, and the third auburn; so she called her daughter Tricolore, which shows that her Majesty had a very fine sense of distributive justice.

The King, who was not a good king, because he was only a good man, thought he had hit upon a brilliant idea in proposing to immure his daughter in a nunnery. The Queen objected, saying that she would never allow it, for fear her daughter would learn expediency before she discovered pleasure. The Monarch said nothing to this because he did not understand it; nor, I imagine, was he the only one; but five or six courtiers were seen to smile, which seemed to show that they appreciated subtlety. Some stupid people are lucky in their laughter: chance often makes them pass for wits.

Tricolore was brought up at Court; she was fortunate enough to have the gift of pleasing, because no one attempted to teach it to her; her education was neglected; no one ever took the trouble to break down her naturalness; she was simple and ingenuous, though she was not lovable, and yet desired passionately to be loved. Women thought her straitlaced, men thought she had propensities, and the Queen, who was beginning to be jealous of her, considered it high time that she was married and taken away. Consequently her name appeared amongst the "matrimonial advertisements" in the papers—with what result we shall see.

Chapter II

One Way of Granting Interviews

The Queen received a large number of Ambassadors concerning the Princess's marriage. However, no question of her appearance or of her disposition was ever entered into; no one wanted either to see her or to become acquainted with her: very careful inquiries were made as to the extent of her revenues; her portrait was never asked for, but every one wanted a detailed inventory of her dowry.

The Queen, on her side, had the foresight to take precautions that were every bit as judicious for her daughter's happiness: she was greatly tempted to give her to the son of the King of Tonquin, because his Ambassador was so handsome and well-set-up. She was just about to decide in his favor, when Prince Tactful craved the favor of an audience. The Queen, who always preserved her dignity, rouged herself, put on her patches, and reclined upon her little curtained bed to receive him with characteristic coquetry.

"Great Queen," said the Prince with a deep bow, "I am afraid that I am lacking in respect to your Majesty."

"That would be strange," retorted the Queen; "others might take offense at your opening, but I do not find it at all offensive."

"Madam," pursued the Prince, "I have a favor to beg of you; and it is you whom I am asking, not the King. I am the son of the Fairy Slyness."

"So far as I can see," said the Queen, "you take after her; moreover, you look interesting; you have large dark eyes and I would wager that you are incapable of bad behavior."

"I always behave well," returned the Prince, "whenever it is possible to do so. Ah, madam!" he continued with a sigh, "how charming Tricolore is!"

"She is not a bad child," observed the Queen; "but she is very ignorant as yet: I may be wrong, but I think that if I were a man little girls would bore me. I see, however, that they are becoming fashionable; no one seems to have any taste or any morals nowadays."

"It is because I have both taste and morals," said the Prince, "that I have designs on the Princess."

"Designs?" interrupted the Queen. "What do you mean by 'designs' on my daughter? Now you are beginning to be lacking in respect for me."

"That is the last thing I want you to

think," replied Tactful; "I only want to prove to your Majesty . . ."

"That you are ignorant of the ways of the world," interrupted the Queen sharply. "I see that all you want is tamely to become Tricolore's husband; you do not do yourself justice; really, Prince, you are worthy of a better fate than that."

At this point the Queen made a movement which revealed her leg, which was a charming one; the Prince was young and susceptible; the Queen took due note of this, and pursued the conversation as follows:

"And yet you seem to me to be no fool."

The Prince's gaze was riveted on the leg.

"Really, madam," he told her, "the more I look at you, the more do I see the resemblance between you and your daughter."

"Yes, that is quite possible," agreed the Queen. "And you are really bent upon marrying her?"

"I will confess," exclaimed the Prince, "that it is my only ambition."

The Queen took the warmth of the day as a pretext for throwing off her neckerchief.

"Well," she promised, "we must arrange an interview."

"Madam," said the Prince, "I have the honor of being known to the Princess; I have occasionally paid my addresses to her, and I think I can flatter myself that she does not object to this step I am taking; so that it seems no purpose can be served by an interview."

"You are very inexperienced," returned the Queen. "I am sure you have

never seen my daughter except in public; on such occasions conversation can
only turn on general subjects: it is impossible to study one another and to become acquainted: you must see each
other alone."

The Prince, quite carried away, thoroughly agreed and said, delightedly:

"Yes, I see now, madam, that an interview is essential."

"It is taking place now," said the
Queen, looking meaningly at the Prince.

He seemed astonished, and looked
round on all sides for Tricolore.

"My daughter has every confidence
in me," resumed the Queen; "I am her
other self; I represent her, and she will
accept you if you appeal to me. My only
fear," she went on, with an affectation
of modesty, "is that my daughter may
not suit you."

The Prince divined the Queen's intentions, and saw that Tricolore would never be his unless he fell in with them. As the Queen was still quite attractive, he hesitated no longer, and expressed himself as follows:

"This method of having interviews only increases my happiness."

At the same time he pressed the Queen's hand. She returned the pressure and remarked:

"Really, Prince, I think my daughter will like you very much."

"I am sure," said he eagerly, "that my whole happiness depends upon her."

"She is very charmed with the way the interview is shaping," continued the Queen.

Tactful began to think that his ordeal was at an end.

"I may flatter myself, then," he

asked, breathing more freely, "that the wedding may take place?"

"Yes, of course," replied the Queen; "your characters suit one another admirably. But you know as well as I do that Great Personages are always married by procuration, and I have taken upon myself the procuration of my daughter."

It was impossible for Tactful to misconstrue the meaning of this statement: he had embarked on this enterprise, and it would have been hopeless for him to have hesitated for a moment. So he was faithless—because of his love. Conversation ceased, and was replaced by the semblance of Pleasure. The Queen spoke only in monosyllables. At last, with something like a sigh, she said:

"Oh, Prince! dear Prince! Do marry my daughter again!"

Chapter III

She did not Expect This

The Queen took the Prince along to find Tricolore.

"Well, my daughter," she said to her, "you must admit that you have enjoyed yourself."

Tricolore blushed; the Prince grew embarrassed; the Queen was bewildered.

"I see," exclaimed the Princess, "that Prince Tactful has belied his name. He seems to have told you everything!"

The Prince regained his calm and admitted that the Princess and he had indeed come to an understanding, but that it had really resulted in a very unsatisfactory affair.

"Apparently," said the Queen, "you have managed to see her by herself.

What was her Maid of Honor doing at the time?"

"I would wager," replied Tactful, "that she was doing what I imagine your own frequently does."

"I insist," continued the Queen, "on hearing the whole story of this escapade."

"I am afraid it will not take long," said Tactful with a sigh: "I was fortunate enough to find the Princess left to her own devices one evening; she was reading the latest novel; I was alarmed lest this should make her dissatisfied with love, so I made her a little speech about the affections, to which she seemed to pay the most careful attention. Flattering myself that I had aroused her interest, I took it upon myself to overcome her shyness; I described the state of my heart to her; I saw that she wished to interrupt me, but her natural politeness, which doubtless, madam, she inherits from you, made her let me finish. I made so bold as to kiss her hand, which she allowed me to do, only because she saw that this favor could lead to nothing."

"What?" said the Queen. "You stopped there?"

"Yes, madam," replied Tactful. "Since the Princess is not so well versed as your Majesty in the ways of the world, she does not know how to do the honors of her house as well as you do."

"That is just as well," interrupted the Queen. "The wedding shall take place."

Accordingly she gave the necessary orders; she arranged for the refreshments, ordered the coaches and the dresses, and had the invitation cards printed. The King was amazed at the news. He had, of course, read it in the Court Circular, but he never believed anything he saw there. He summoned the Queen and the Princess, and asked them if they took him for the King of Diamonds.

"No, Sire," the Queen retorted, "for I often have quite good fun with him. Besides, in your heart you know perfectly well that you have no rights at all over the Princess. The wedding will take place; I have consulted the oracles."

"And I assure you that it will not take place," cried the Fairy Rancor, who suddenly appeared on the scene in a sulky, with her son, Prince Potiron, on the back seat. "I intend the Princess to bestow her hand upon my handsome son here!"

"We shall see about that," exclaimed

the Fairy Slyness, unexpectedly arriving in a cabriolet drawn by six foxes.

"Let us combine forces, madam," said the Queen immediately. "I rely upon your protection."

"You shall most certainly have it," promised the Fairy Slyness, "and I will give you a very striking proof of it at once."

At the same time she pushed the Queen against the wall, and touched her with her wand, whereupon the Queen of the Patagonians became a beautiful tapestry figure. Tricolore screamed; the Fairy Rancor made a face; Prince Potiron laughed loudly; Prince Tactful asked a question; and the King of the Patagonians expressed his gratitude.

How delightful the events in a story always are! The metamorphosis of the Queen was an act of High Diplomacy;

the Fairy Rancor's displeasure was a
proof of that. The Fairy Slyness was
triumphant. Nevertheless, her triumph
was to be short-lived, for the quarrel between these two Powers was to be the
cause of many conflicting and annoying
adventures.

"Oh, my son," exclaimed the Fairy
Slyness, "what pleasures, what sor-
rows, what happiness, what misfortunes! How will you ever be able to
bear them all? Let us go to consult our
Grand Instructor."

Chapter IV

Which does not Reveal Much

The Grand Instructor had lived for some time with a Fairy who made him pay nothing for his board, though she did not lodge him for nothing. She was a little old Fairy with a youthful complexion, a serene outlook, and a young heart. She suppressed her passions and paraded her tastes, of which she had many. She applauded at the French opera, but gave only Italian concerts in her own Palace. She had two chefs, one for old-fashioned and one for new-fangled cooking. The first was for all her clever friends, the second to cook suppers for pretty women. She never left her Palace except to go to the Theater; she never visited other people, but she kept open house herself; she was convinced that one should not go out into the social whirl when one is no longer young enough to play one's part in it, but that one should attract it to one's own house to study the people who compose it. She liked serious conversation with intelligent people in the morning, and dissipation with young people in the evening. She was sure of not being bored if she saw others amusing themselves; and if pleasure had left her behind, she at least had the skill to bring its perspective nearer to her.

As she dreaded loneliness, all her Palaces abutted on the several houses of the King of Patagonia. She was one of the Fairies in attendance at the Court. Not to have been presented to her was not to be in the fashion. She thought that was the Fairy Slyness's only motive in bringing Prince Tactful to her: however, she thoroughly approved of him, and told him that his appearance was more fashionable than his name. The conversation opened on general topics, which are friends that never fail one in an emergency: it then turned to the topic of the day; the Fairy Slyness said that the Queen had been changed into a tapestry figure, at which the little old woman exclaimed:

"All the better!"

"Madam," said the Prince, "I must confess that I am not shrewd enough to see the aptness of your comment. I love Tricolore passionately."

"All the better!" repeated the Fairy.

"I rather fear," continued Tactful, "that it is all the worse. The Queen approved of my love; now she is no longer in a condition to give me her approval."

"All the better!" said the Fairy again.

"I do not understand you," said the Prince. "Her father is a good man, but he is weak; the Fairy Rancor will make him give her the Princess for her son Potiron."

"All the better!" cried the Fairy loudly. "All the better, my dear boy! At your age one's feelings are very violent, but one is not very far-seeing, unless one be a privileged mortal like the Grand Instructor. He is a friend of the gods and turns everything to account. He beholds his glory in the past, his pleasure in the present, and his happiness in the future. Nothing distresses him, nothing discourages him. That is why he is called the Grand Instructor of all that is for the best in the world. I will fetch him for you: he will console you."

"Madam," said the Prince to his

mother, when they were alone, "do you know this All-the-Better gentleman?"

"Yes, my son," replied the Fairy; "he is a holy man who does a great deal of good: he places himself at every one's disposal. If he sees a woman who is no longer young, he says: 'All the better!' and perhaps he is not far wrong. In a woman of a certain age, more is for the better than one thinks. If he sees one who still clings to the simplicity of child-hood, he never fails to say: 'Ah! All the better!' And I do not think, my son, that you will find it difficult to guess the reason. If he is told that a woman is madly in love with her husband, he im-mediately exclaims: 'All the better! To love one's husband one must have a very sensitive soul: that woman will one day be an ornament to Society, and it will be an asset to her.' If he is told that a woman loathes her husband, 'Ah! How very much for the best that is!' says the holy man, rolling a kindly eye. 'It shows that the lady has a very nice judgment; I am sure she has a beautiful nature'."

"You seem to have a very clear idea of his," observed the Prince.

Tact prevented him from saying any more, and at this point the little Fairy returned, accompanied by the Grand Instructor.

Chapter V

On which the Prince is not Spoilt

The Grand Instructor was a man of about six feet in height, well-set-up, and a little heavy in the leg, though this became him very well. He had broad, well-knit shoulders, beautiful teeth, level eyes, and a generous nose. I doubt whether he was very witty, but his physical qualities were worth more than any fine phrases.

Naturally enough, when he had been warned that the Fairy Slyness had come to consult him, he assumed his prophetic expression. He bowed slightly to her, and looked at the Prince as if he had been an Acolyte.

"My lord," the Fairy addressed him respectfully, "your reputation is so world-wide that I have decided to ask

your advice. You know how kind I have
been to the Queen?"

"Yes," he replied coldly, "I am aware
of everything: your son's happiness is
your only object, and he is very much in
love; that is all simple enough. He
wants to get married, which is dull; and
he wants his wife to be good, which is
rather droll."

"Then she will not be?" asked the
Prince eagerly.

"You or I will prevent it," replied the
Pontiff. "You want to be married and
not to be deceived: that would be something quite unique. Your mother, who
saved her own husband from such a ridiculous situation, foresaw the misery
to which your prejudices would bring
you, and provided against them by the
cleverly inspired metamorphosis of the
Queen."

"I do not understand you," interrupted the Prince impatiently; "your remarks are too obscure."

"I quite agree with you," remarked the little Fairy. "Oh! our Instructor has a very fine intellect!"

"Touching the matter of the spell cast upon the Queen," continued the Prince in high excitation.

"Not so fast," said the Grand Instructor. "That is no business of yours. It is not for you to break it, but for me."

"And how do you make that out?" asked the Prince.

"How do I make that out?" replied the Grand Instructor ironically. "You remember how you interviewed Tricolore with the Queen?"

The Prince flushed, and the two Fairies smiled. The Priest continued as follows:

"You remember how you conducted that interview, do you not? Answer me truthfully."

"Well, yes, of course I do, but what does that prove?"

"That proves," replied the Grand Instructor, "that your skill lies in granting interviews and mine in breaking spells. Every one has a different gift. I will say no more."

"I consent," said the Prince, "but at least relieve me of a cruel doubt. Which of us two, Potiron or I, will be fortunate enough to possess the Princess?"

"I will reveal the matter clearly to you," replied the Prophet in his characteristic cocksure fashion.

He then strode three times round the room, traced out three times three crescents, that is to say nine, raised his eyes thrice in the direction of the moon, made three faces, threw three capers, laughed thrice, and then pronounced the following mysterious and infallible judgment:

"Prince Tactful will get Princess Tricolore, and yet he will not get her; all the better for her! Prince Potiron will get Princess Tricolore, and yet he will not get her; all the better for her and for me!"

"Ah, what a clever man!" exclaimed the Fairy Slyness.

"Ah, what a great man!" exclaimed the little old woman.

"Ah, what an idiot!" exclaimed Prince Tactful.

Then the Instructor, still polite in spite of being inspired, bowed low to the Fairy Slyness, shook hands with the little old woman and took leave of the Prince, saying to him:

"Always remain thoroughly enlightened."

Chapter VI
More for the Best

The Prince remained very stupid, nor is
he the first charming person to whom
that has happened. His mother was herself very embarrassed, but the Grand
Instructor was very far from finding
himself in like case, for the Fairy Rancor
was awaiting him in his study with Princess Tricolore. They had come accompanied by the King of the Patagonians
and the handsome Prince Potiron,
though they might have chosen a better
escort.

No sooner was the Queen metamorphosed than the King considered
himself to be capable of deciding everything, because there was no longer any-
body to dictate to him. He opposed
the Fairy Rancor and insisted on the

wedding between Tricolore and Prince Tactful, pleading the wishes of the Queen.

"If that be all," answered the Fairy, "I can soon ease your mind of that little scruple. Do you remember that Fate decreed that the Queen should only be empowered to marry those children of whom you are the father?"

"That may be so," said the King: "I do not wish to discuss it; but in this very delicate matter perhaps your son will be like me."

Potiron, who knew something of the world, replied politely:

"You seem to think that every one is as lazy as yourself. I will undertake to be the father of my own children, but I want to know if any one is going to interfere in my affairs, and that is why we must consult the Grand Instructor."

As he caught sight of him in the distance, Potiron called out:

"Divine Oracle, I want to get married!"

"And I do not want to," added Tricolore.

"Well, then," observed the Grand Instructor, "you are both right."

"We have come to ask you," said the Fairy Rancor, "what is going to happen about it."

"A great many things," replied the inspired man. "I must first of all warn you that the Princess's husband and her lover will be two different persons. Pay heed to me. The Future is unfolding itself before my vision—

"Prince Tactful will reap the first-fruits of the Princess; all the better for her! Prince Tactful will not have

the first-fruits of the Princess; all the better for me!"

"You are wanting in common sense," declared Tricolore at once; "can you not see that the two oracles contradict each other?"

"They are none the less both true," replied the Prophet.

"I must expect, then," said Potiron, "that if I marry this young lady I shall not be first in the field?"

"That requires explaining," answered the Grand Instructor. "She will bring you her first-fruits—so much is certain—but not before she has had seventeen children."

"This good fellow ought to be sent to the Mad House," said Tricolore.

"Do not scoff at him," interrupted the King. "That is his way of talking."

The Grand Instructor recovered his enthusiasm.

"I see still more things happening," he went on, "which I am sure will make you shudder, but which are all for the best."

These words, far from frightening Tricolore, reassured her; she flattered herself that Prince Tactful's happiness was one of the things that were all for the best. The holy man read this thought in her face, and pronounced these terrible words:

"I know what you think; but, oh, Princess! How you deceive yourself! You will cause your lover's death, and it will be all the better for him."

"Oh, Heaven!" cried Tricolore. "Can this be possible?"

"But," said Potiron, "this hardly gives her a very charming character. If she treats a lover so, think what a reception her husband will get!"

"Her husband," the Prophet went on, "will escape with the colic."

"Ah! I can hesitate no longer," exclaimed Potiron; "she shall be my wife immediately."

"Oh, Fairy Slyness!" cried the Princess as loudly as she could. "Oh, Fairy Slyness, will you allow it? Oh, Fairy Slyness, help me!"

The Fairy Slyness was artfully listening at the door with her son. She came in at once, muttered a few words, and placed her hands over Tricolore's pretty face, turning her into a nice little hen-partridge.

"All the better!" observed the Grand Instructor.

At the same time the Fairy touched Prince Tactful with her little finger, and he, as you have foreseen, became a cock-partridge, proud and full of love.

"All the better!" the Grand Instructor observed once more.

Our lovers' joy can be imagined; but judge their despair when the Fairy Rancor seized hold of Tricolore saying:

"Gently, my darling, gently; you shall be put into a cage; and as you are very much in love you will make an admirable decoy bird. You will often call, and Master Tactful will inevitably come to you; my handsome son Potiron will hide himself, which is one of the things he does best; I will give him a good musket and he will kill his rival, the cock, and then I will see to it that his marriage is celebrated."

The King of the Patagonians, recollecting that the Oracle had predicted that the Princess would cause her

lover's death, could not repress a sigh
as he said:

"Ah, Poor Prince! That is the end of
you."

"And as for Tricolore," added the
Grand Instructor, "it will be all the better for her."

Chapter VII

A Short One, which will Perhaps be Found too Long

Prince Tactful, after becoming a cock-partridge, was less affectionate but more ardent: which is as it should be. Princess Tricolore, shut up in her cage, felt, beyond any possibility of doubt, that she would not play the prude. Prince Potiron prepared his weapon, whereupon the Fairy Rancor had a deep hole dug.

The brilliant sun began to set, and the evening grew calm, reassuring the dwellers in the plains, inviting them to make the best of their good health. Potiron set out, and on his arrival took up his position; the cage was placed ten feet away from him, and the Fairy Rancor withdrew to a distance. Tricolore,

who knew exactly what was in the air,
determined not to make even the slight-
est sound; but with partridges, just as
with many excellent people, Nature
often gets the best of it in spite of the
most elaborate precautions.

Tricolore, who was deliciously con-
scious of the proximity of her mate,
began quite involuntarily to squawk.
Whereupon Tactful shook his wings,
preened himself, stretched himself to his
full height and threw out his chest; he
strutted round the cage, sprang on top of
it, hopped down again, postured before
the hen-partridge, put his head between
the bars, offered her his beak, and began
to make love noises.

Beside himself with rage, Potiron took
aim and pulled the trigger; but like master, like weapon: Potiron's weapon just
made a click. He hastened to reprime

it. It clicked again. It would do nothing but click.

"Ah, cursed weapon! Filthy gimcrack!" he cried, foaming at the mouth with fury.

Whilst he was wasting his time the cock was by no means wasting his: he managed to lift the door of the cage, and enjoyed himself to the full under the very nose of his rival. Potiron could not climb out of his hole, for his body was too heavy and his legs too short. He began to cry out at the top of his voice both in anger and exasperation:

"Ho! Mother, my dear mother! Come and stop this ruffian!"

The Fairy Rancor made a single bound, and had already laid hands on Tactful when the Fairy Slyness (who was present, though she couldn't be seen) immediately made her son as in-

visible as herself. Rancor looked for
him in vain.

"Madam," said Potiron, "I do not
entertain too high an opinion of this
Princess's modesty."

"I will punish her for it," promised
the Fairy; "but we must respect her condition."

She was taken back to the Palace and
laid seventeen eggs, of which not one
was addled. So Tricolore had seventeen children in her first child-bed
without having lost her first-fruits as a
Princess. One of the prophecies of the
Grand Instructor had come true. As
soon as the children were fully fledged,
they were set at liberty, and the Fairy
Slyness gave their mother back her
natural shape.

"Ah, madam!" she cried, in a trans-
port of joy, "how much I owe to you!

But, I beg of you, tell me what has become of your son?"

At this question the Fairy Slyness grew sad, and after a moment's silence answered as follows:

"You will hear about that only too soon. The Grand Instructor never makes a mistake. You cannot avoid being the cause of your lover's death: and on the very evening on which he dies you will be compelled to wed Potiron."

Tricolore broke into lamentations; but the Fairy Slyness, who foresaw that this would not be amusing, left her alone, and was quite right to do so. We will follow her example and leave the Princess to her reflections. The things one says to oneself are not always fit for the ears of others.

Chapter VIII

On which the Grand Instructor Gets into Difficulties

Let it suffice to say that Tricolore, after carefully considering every means of avoiding the misfortunes in store for her, made up her mind never to enter the Fairy Rancor's garden, so as never to meet Tactful.

"For," she mused, very sensibly, "if I never see him, it will be very difficult for me to kill him."

From which it appears that the Princess possessed a very logical mind.

On the following day, which was a very warm one, Tricolore went for a stroll in the cool of the evening: she came upon a beautiful stretch of green grass, and could not resist the impulse to lie down beneath the spreading

branches of an old oak, where she fell
fast asleep. You think I am going to
bring Prince Tactful on the scene; but
you are wrong, I am only going to bring
on the Grand Instructor; but the tale
loses nothing for that. Chance led him
to that spot; he had to deliver a sermon
on the discomforts of chastity, and he
had come to prepare it in this lonely
wood. What a superb text for him to
find! Tricolore fast asleep! I do not
know in exactly what attitude the Princess was lying, but the Priest exclaimed:

"Heavens! How lovely that is!"

He hid himself behind a bush, afraid
of making a noise, though he could not
help tapping the ground with his foot.
He was trembling with excitement. His
delight was momentarily increasing,
when he heard the Princess breathe an
audible sigh, and saw her stir in her

sleep. His joy was seraphic, but every nerve in his body thrilled as he saw Tricolore's eyes half-open, and he heard her say, softly:

"Ah! How that tickles!"

She seemed to fall asleep again, but a minute later she woke up completely, exclaiming:

"Oh! It's burning me!"

Thinking she was alone, she began to search, and found a glow-worm hidden in the grass, and most happily placed.

An astute reader will easily have guessed, from the position taken up by the glow-worm, that it was none other than Prince Tactful, metamorphosed by his mother. The Princess seized it and doubted what it really was.

"Well!" she cried, "it is amusing to think that was what excited me so much. However, I must see if it has stung me."

But at this critical moment the Grand Instructor felt the situation to be too much for him, and in spite of himself, he exclaimed:

"Ouf! I can stand no more!"

Poor Tricolore was seized with fear and shame.

"Well, sir!" she said. "Who would have thought it of you! The clergy seem to want to intrude everywhere!"

The Grand Instructor, who was entirely engrossed in his own thoughts, replied with a sigh:

"Ah! How lucky that glow-worm is!"

"Is that what you call a glow-worm?" asked the Princess.

"Yes," replied the Instructor. "I admire the wisdom of Nature, who has set a spark of fire on his tail."

"Yes, it is strange," replied Tricolore; "and what do you conclude from that?"

"That in this luminous insect," replied the Prophet, "is perhaps hidden a lover."

At the word "lover," Tricolore trembled; she fell into a reverie, with her eyes fixed on the glow-worm, and then said in a sympathetic voice:

"Poor little thing, how pretty it is! And do you know," she went on, "when I think of the place where it was found, do you know that you may be right, and perhaps it is a lover."

"Make no mistake," said the Grand Instructor; "that star is merely a spark that Love has let fall from his torch. Madam," he continued, "be good enough to squeeze it a little to see if it wags its tail."

Tricolore, out of curiosity, pressed it between finger and thumb, but to her surprise and horror she felt it crush, and suddenly she heard the voice of Prince Tactful saying:

"Ah, Tricolore, I am dying by your hand; how glad I am!"

The Prince expired, the Princess swooned, and the Grand Instructor exclaimed:

"Victory! Victory! Tricolore has killed her lover! All the better for him, all the better for her, and all the better for me!"

Chapter IX
And so Does Prince Potiron

When this affair became known, the King of the Patagonians sent our heralds to announce the wedding of the Princess with Prince Potiron: there was nothing now to prevent it. The marriage feast was held, and every one ate more than they spoke, though they spoke more than they thought. The fare was sumptuous, the jests were coarse, every one grew tired, and the King, thoroughly enjoying himself, announced in a voice full of knowingness that it was time to lead the happy pair to their apartment. I will pass over the ceremony. The Prince seemed stupid, the Princess despondent; nor did appearances lie. The Fairy Rancor laughed as hate laughs, and the Grand

Instructor made a fine harangue; but that was not the best thing he was to do.

Arrived in the nuptial chamber, the lovely Tricolore put on the most entrancing deshabille; but she was made even more charming and desirable by her embarrassment and her blushes. On occasions of this sort modesty always pays tribute to passion.

Potiron did not cut so fine a figure in his night-cap. However, he wore a handsome flesh-colored dressing-gown. The King thought that the moment had come to leave them: he dismissed the company and took it upon himself to withdraw, leaning on two pages, after making some gross remark which he mistook for wit.

Just as every one was leaving, a voice was heard pronouncing these words:

"It is not all over yet."

"Madam," said Potiron immediately, "allow me to contradict that statement."

Tricolore preserved a modest silence which seemed to show submission to her husband. He was about to take advantage of this when the Princess made a face, heaved a sigh and shifted her position. Potiron, full of concern, contained his ardor and asked her what the matter was.

"My lord," she replied, "it is something very strange."

"Do you feel a pain anywhere?" pursued Potiron.

"My lord, it is something more embarrassing than painful."

"Madam, allow me to look."

"I dare not," she protested. "If you only knew where it was."

"By your answer you tell me where it is," returned Potiron.

At the same time he ventured to look; but what was his amazement when he found a full-blown rose surrounded by thorns.

"Oh! What a lovely rose!" he cried. "Is it, madam, by any chance a birthmark?"

"Sir," replied the Princess, "I think it has only just come there."

"That is very strange," observed Potiron; "I am either being played a trick or paid a compliment. But there is something written there too. Perhaps it is a motto? Allow me to fetch a light. The type is very small: it looks to me like Elzevir."

Potiron went to fetch a candlestick, but on his return he found that the ornament had changed. The rose and thorns had disappeared: their place had been taken by two fingers which made horns at him. Potiron flew into a rage.

"Madam!" he cried. "You have a lover, and there are his fingers!"

"My lord, what is possessing you? You are insulting me!"

"Madam, be good enough to stand up, to see if it will change."

The Princess arose, but the two fingers remained. Potiron tried to think: whenever he did so the results were always unfortunate; but this time he had a new experience.

"Princess," he went on, cheerfully, "all this is only a game. It is only a poor joke of the Fairy Slyness, who wants to spoil my pleasure by making me suspicious of you. I may observe that those two fingers cannot prevent me from giving you proofs of my respect for you. They will, no doubt, disappear when I have scorned them."

Whereupon he experienced an untimely desire (he never seemed to have timely ones), and wished to satisfy it; but the two fingers immediately became a pair of pincers which nipped him pitilessly. He began to scream, and his torment was increased by the fact that at that moment the Princess, by an involuntary impulse, began to walk backwards as quickly as a swift runner could have done had he been running away from him.

"Ho! Madam!" he cried. "You are crazy; you don't know what you are doing. Stop!"

"I cannot stop, sir!" she replied, dragging him round and round the room faster and faster.

"Madam!" screamed Potiron. "This is too much; I shall never be of any use to you all my life!"

At length, however, after a good quarter of an hour, Tricolore fell on a sofa and Potiron, finding himself free, rolled to the ground and lost his senses.

Chapter X

One Method of Breaking a Spell

Potiron recovered consciousness: which was not recovering much. He opened his eyes, looked at the Princess, and made the following sensible remark:

"Madam, I would much prefer you to lead me by the nose."

The Princess, who had also somewhat recovered, felt a desire to laugh; she controlled herself, however, and made no reply.

"Are they still there?" Potiron went on.

"I am afraid so," answered Tricolore.

"We had better see," said the Prince.

He found them there more than ever, like a pair of calipers, with the words: These are for you. They were quite huge.

"I am very glad to have found them again," exclaimed Potiron; "I have in my pocket a pair of scissors given to me by my mother: they possess the virtue of being able to cut through anything enchanted."

The test succeeded: he cut off the two fingers; but immediately the rose and the thorns took their place, accompanied by these words: These are for him. He carried out the same operation on this new spell, and the two fingers reappeared, still with: These are for you.

"Madam," said the Prince, "this place seems to me never to be empty."

"That is the horoscope that has always been cast about it," observed Tricolore.

"What I cannot understand," pursued Potiron, "is the meaning of these two mottoes: These are for you, and

These are for him. I feel that there is a great deal underlying them, but I do not understand it."

"The first motto," replied the Princess, "seems to be the less obscure of the two; and the symbol seems to make it still more easily understandable."

The Fairies Rancor and Slyness arrived during this discussion.

"My son," said Rancor, "I know you are in a difficulty; but it is not nearly over yet."

"Is that all you can do to get me out of it?" retorted Potiron. "Can you explain to me what this rose and its appendages mean?"

"That is my wedding present," put in the Fairy Slyness.

"For a present of that kind it is very appropriately situated," observed Potiron. "And the two fingers?"

"The two fingers," continued Slyness, "are a present from my son. He
gave them to the Princess and charged
her to give them to you."

"Unfortunately," said the Fairy Rancor, "they will remain there until they
reach their natural destination: it is only
a question of time; however, they will
disappear altogether if they do not prevent you from finding happiness with
the Princess. Make an effort, my dear
son."

"Faith, no!" cried Potiron. "I do not
want to be caught again!" Then, thinking better of it: "I will try," he
said, "once more to break the spell; so,
ladies, will you please be good enough
to withdraw."

And Potiron, with renewed courage,
tried to seize the enchanted rose: his
torments did not deter him. Alas! He

was a victim of his own valor: he found himself enveloped in a thousand Chinese crackers of every conceivable color.

"Fire! Fire!" yelled Potiron.

"My lord," entreated the Princess, "be careful you do not get blistered."

"There is magic in everything that happens here!" screamed Prince Potiron.

"No doubt this is another compliment from the Fairy Slyness," returned the Princess. "There were no fireworks at the wedding festivities: they were reserved for a more fitting occasion; you must admit that the manufacture of fireworks has made great strides in the most unexpected places."

The two Fairies reappeared, saying: "Oh! What a smell of burning!"

"There is good reason for it," replied Potiron. "If the King's Artillery is as well equipped as that of his daughter, I defy any one to take his forts."

"There is a very simple way of removing this obstacle," pursued the Fairy Slyness. "You, of course, know that the Queen, your mother-in-law, has been changed into a tapestry figure?"

"Well," said Potiron, "how does that affect me? I know quite well that it is one of your jests, but I do not see the object of it."

"Then I will tell you," said Slyness in a kindly voice. "It is natural for me to take the side of my son, for he was in love with the Princess."

"Faith!" interrupted Potiron. "I had sufficient proof of that on the decoy-bird evening; but, thank Heavens, that little fellow is no more!"

"He will come back again," answered the Fairy. "I now come to the main point. Seeing, then, that my son was in love with the Princess, and that you had the right to marry her, I at least tried to prevent you from enjoying your happiness, and to succeed in this I thought it necessary to cast a spell upon the Queen and another upon Tricolore. The second spell cannot be broken until after the first one: so that you will never remove the barrier that deprives you of the Princess except by giving the Queen back her natural shape."

"I am sure you are very clever," replied Potiron, "but I think you are lacking in common sense. How can I possibly contrive that the Queen should cease to be a tapestry figure?"

"Quite easily," answered the Fairy; "simply by treating her as you wanted to treat her daughter."

"Who? Me?" cried the Prince

sharply. "To have dealings with a Queen in high-warp tapestry? I would not dream of such a thing!"

"Really," urged Rancor, "you must do the Queen of the Patagonians this favor; otherwise some one else will break the spell on the Princess."

"But truly," exclaimed Potiron, "I swear to you upon my honor that it is quite impossible!"

"Very well, then!" said the Fairy Slyness coldly; "let the Grand Instructor be sent for."

Chapter XI

Which will Surprise Nobody

The Grand Instructor arrived in a flowing robe, and asked the ladies what they required of his feeble powers.

"It is a mere bagatelle," explained Potiron: "it is a question of treating the Queen as you always treat pretty women."

"You wish to put me to the test?" asked the Pontiff.

"Oh, well, even if that were so," replied Potiron, "the test would only do you honor."

"My lord," observed the Grand Instructor, "I know too well the respect I owe you."

"I will absolve you from that!" retorted Potiron. "I am quite aware that the tall figure over there is my mother-

in-law; but you may be wanting in respect for her as much as you like without
any protest from me."

"You do not understand me," returned the Instructor; "I shall not at-
tempt to break the spell on the Queen.
I have no wish to enter into competition
with you. To break that spell is your
business: mine is to break the one on the
Princess. Allow me to proceed with my
small task."

"I beg your pardon, your rever-
ence?" cried the Prince sharply.

"My lord," put in the Fairy Slyness,
with a look that showed she was dying
to laugh, "Fate, by a strange freak, has
decreed that these two spells shall be
bound together. When one is broken,
the other will be broken also. Only you
can succeed in breaking that on the
Queen: and if you do not wish to avail

yourself of such a rare privilege, the honor of breaking the spell on the Princess belongs by right to our Instructor."

"A fig for that!" sneered Potiron.

"I want to gather the rose, my lord," said the holy man; "beware of the words: These are for him."

"Well, then," said Potiron, "I am he."

"My lord," returned the Grand Instructor, "I think you are in error; you are you. The first motto is for you, and the two fingers will come to you sooner or later; but I am sure that the rose will be for me."

With these words the Grand Instructor turned to the Princess. Potiron clung to him to stop him; but the Instructor pronounced this conjuration:

"Invisible Powers, subject to my commands, stretch across this place a

Holy Curtain to separate me from the profane!"

Immediately the room was divided into two parts by a rich curtain of Genoese velvet. Potiron remained with the two Fairies on the side of the Tapestry Queen, and the Instructor found himself alone with the Princess on the side containing the bed.

Potiron, like all little men, became furious: he tried to crawl under the curtain; he screamed out at the top of his voice:

"You wait! Only just you wait, you vile priest!"

"That is just what you must not do!" cried Tricolore.

These words increased the storm in the poor Prince's brain:

"Ah! Accursed monkey that you are,"

98

he raved, "you will have me to deal with!"

"And in the meantime," observed the Fairy Slyness, "it seems that the Princess will have the Grand Instructor to deal with."

"My only consolation," said Potiron, "is that he will at least scratch himself. A little silence, ladies, I beg of you; we must know how he fares; the matter deserves our attention."

At the same time he pressed his ear to the curtain and heard the following unexpected dialogue:

"Oh! What joy!" exclaimed the Grand Instructor.

"Joy?" interrupted Potiron. "Why, the man must be crazy! Let us hear some more."

"Oh! You are hurting me!" cried the Princess.

"I am beside myself!" pursued the servant of the gods.

"I am going to faint," went on Tricolore.

"Dearest Princess, adorable Princess, truly divine beauty," stammered the Grand Instructor brokenly, "be brave for just one moment more."

"Ah! I am dead!" cried the Princess, with a piercing scream.

The spell was broken, the curtain disappeared, and the tapestry Queen threw herself on the Grand Instructor's neck, saying to him:

"My lord, how grateful I am to your Eminence!" Then, turning to Potiron, she continued: "I must congratulate you, my son-in-law."

"My son," said the Fairy Rancor, "you are not the only one."

"My lord," said the Grand Instructor

to Potiron, "I shall always be at your orders whenever you feel inclined to add to the perquisites of my poor emoluments."

Potiron remained alone with the Princess: she had not yet recovered consciousness. To revive her, he tried to take her pulse (every one to his own methods). She apparently thought it was the Grand Instructor who was doing so. She pressed his hand, saying:

"Ah! My dear Father."

And at the same time she opened her eyes.

"What! Is it you, sir," she went on. "What are you doing here?"

"All that I can, madam," replied Potiron, with a great deal of truth.

Tricolore grew confused and the Prince was embarrassed; but he was even more curious than embarrassed.

"Aha!" he cried in astonishment. "The rose and the thorns have disappeared; but, really, that man possesses some excellent secrets; apparently it was this excision which made you so happy?"

"Precisely," replied Tricolore.

"I can well believe it," he observed; "but that does not prevent its being a beautifully carried out operation; but what did he do with it all?"

"My lord," said the Princess, "he took it away to place it in his Natural History cabinet."

"After all, that is only fair," reflected Potiron. "That is no doubt what he meant when he thanked me for increasing his perquisites. To be quite frank, I am far from being displeased. It is a good job done: and now I feel quite sleepy."

Chapter XII

Which Borders on the Pathetic

The next morning was devoted to cere-
monial toilet. When Tricolore had dis-
posed of this—after she had suffered all
the visits of the Court Ladies, who on
that day made more parade of their at-
tractions and were more simpering in
their expressions than usual; after she
had borne all the arch looks of the Queen
and of the Fairy Slyness; after she had
listened to the fatuous ambiguities of all
the courtiers—she decided to devote the
afternoon to reverie and repose. What
can a Princess dream about? About
what she loves, of course. Consequently Prince Tactful played a large
part in the Princess's thoughts. (We
shall soon see what comes of thoughts.)
She imagined she had killed her dear

Prince: she brooded on her misfortune in having had a lover who was dead, and in having a husband who could never be alive, without her being any more a widow because of it.

The profundity of these meditations occupied her until dusk, when it was announced to her that a young man desired ardently to see her, if only for a moment's interview.

"A young man!" she exclaimed in surprise. "A young man?"

"Yes, madam," was the reply; "he does not appear to be more than twenty."

"His youth touches me," she observed; "let him be shown in. I do not want the lights lit yet."

The young man was ushered into the apartment; but he was seized with a sudden weakness and, leaning against a writing-table, was only able to say in a faint voice: "Ah, mademoiselle!"

The Princess was confused.

"Mademoiselle!" said she. "What do you mean by that?"

"I am dying!" exclaimed the young man; "have you become Potiron's wife?"

"What is this I hear? Oh, Heaven! Have my ears deceived me?" cried Tricolore. "That was the dying voice of the poor glow-worm when it thanked me so gracefully for having crushed it; the more I think of it, the more certain I am. Tell me, do you still possess that precious star?"

"Heaven! Now that you are married, there is no longer any star for me," replied the Prince.

"Alas! I can no longer doubt," cried Tricolore. "It is my Prince himself: he is still alive—It only depends on you to make me love him; but I fear your prejudices. I am afraid of—My lord," Tricolore broke off, "you would be more comfortable seated: you can talk more at your ease if you rest your head."

"I will do so," promised Tactful, "on condition that it does not make yours any calmer."

He took an armchair, and Tricolore lay on a sofa. Tactful resumed the conversation as follows, in a voice at once serious and affectionate:

"Madam, since I must call you that, I am concerned about Potiron."

"I recognize your generosity," said the Princess. "What do you want to do for him?"

"I want to save him trouble," declared Tactful.

The Princess, who had a quick wit,

saw exactly what the Prince was leading up to, and remarked spiritedly:

"My lord, I recognize your delicacy, but I know my duty."

"Does he fulfill his own duty properly?" asked Tactful eagerly.

The Princess made no reply.

"Ah!" continued the Prince, "I see that Potiron acts in the same way that you answer. Is it possible that he does not fall into ecstasy before so much charm?"

And with these words the Prince threw himself at the Princess's feet in humble admiration.

"Prince," she said, "I implore you to rise: your attitude is respectful, but I have been told it is a convenient one for disrespect."

"Do not believe it," urged Tactful, "and try to know me better. My love for you is based on the most profound respect."

"Alas!" sighed Tricolore. "When love starts it pretends to respect, but it lies; when it ends it promises friendship, but it never keeps its word."

"That," said Tactful, "is an epigram which appears rather insincere. Are you already becoming a wit? Tricolore, Tricolore, be guided only by your heart!"

Here he apparently started importuning her, for the Princess said to him sharply:

"Sir, I shall ring the bell!"

"Ah! If only the hour were propitious!" continued Tactful, in the most affectionate voice.

"No, no, I have too much respect for virtue in my heart."

"There was a time," the Prince went

on, "when I should at least have taken second place there."

And with these words he glanced longingly at her and squeezed her hand. Tricolore was much moved, and pleaded thus:

"Ah, Prince, my dear Prince, leave me alone, I beg of you!"

The Prince did not leave her alone, but kissed her in a way that the circumstances seemed to demand.

"This is too much!" cried the Princess. "Leave me at once and never dare to return!"

The Prince was quite abashed, and falteringly said:

"Madam, I will obey you."

He had already reached the antechamber when Tricolore, touched by his distress, felt impelled to call out to him:

"Prince, when shall I see you again?"

"Very soon, madam," he replied, completely recovering himself.

But just then Potiron came in, and Tactful retired, after making her a deep bow. Potiron thought the bow was for him. A husband always appropriates to himself the compliments paid to his wife, and his vanity always meets his wife half-way when she wants to be unfaithful to him.

Chapter XIII

Matters Take a Fresh Turn

Potiron bowed to the Prince with his hand on his stomach, like a banker.

"There is a poor fellow who is altogether too much of a ninny," he remarked to the Princess: "I'll wager you received him coldly, perhaps even sharply, which is not right. I do not at all object to your doing people the honors of my house, so long as you do not give them the pleasures of it."

"That," said Tricolore, "is a privilege which is reserved for you."

Whilst Potiron was drawing these conclusions, the Fairy Slyness was forming a more accurate idea of her son's actions. She guessed from the look in his eyes that if he did not hold happiness within his grasp, he was at

any rate very near to it. He was not be-
having himself like a coxcomb who, even
in framing a denial, is guilty of an in-
discretion; he denied everything with
the effrontery necessary to the occasion,
and lied like a gentleman.

"You do not want to tell me how you
stand with the Princess?" asked the
Fairy. "Then I shall find out in spite of
you. That is all I have to say to you at
this moment."

Accordingly, as soon as she left the
Prince she cast a spell on all husbands,
its effect being to give them an attack of
colic whenever their wives had a weak
moment. I am sure the reader has foreseen an epidemic of stomach-aches.
Tricolore never suspected that Potiron
would be in that case. She was inces-
santly preening herself on her virtue:
she was perpetually grateful to herself

for the harshness with which she had treated her lover: she did not realize that to be so pleased with herself about it showed that she was amazed at it, and that such amazement is the first sign of weakening. True virtue never preens itself on anything. A woman who is indifferent resists, but hardly remembers having done so; an affectionate woman congratulates herself on her refusals, and in congratulating herself she calls to mind the man concerned; she relents, and in the end surrenders. As a general rule, to dwell too much upon defense is to prepare for defeat. However, Tricolore made plans for the most glorious defense. How far it succeeded will shortly be seen.

On the following day Prince Tactful carefully noted when Potiron went out, to fix the moment for his visit.

"Princess," he said, approaching her, "your eyes look tired, which shows me to my sorrow that Potiron spent a good night."

"Prince," she replied, "that is a tone which does not become you. It might have been witty. As it is, it is only rather involved."

"It would not be difficult to explain," said the Prince.

"I will spare you the trouble," said the Princess hurriedly. "What shall we talk about?"

"About you," replied the Prince.

"No, I mistrust that."

"About Potiron?"

"That would bore me."

"About me, then?" suggested the Prince romantically.

"Still less," answered Tricolore sharply. "You would only speak of yourself in order to bring me into the conversation."

"But I want these two things to go together."

"If I am not careful, you will begin again," cried Tricolore. "Let us change the subject. Why, for instance, did your mother change you into a glow-worm? I have never understood her object in doing that."

"It is quite simple," he told her. "You must remember the time when I was a cock-partridge—indeed, madam, it was you who did me the honor to allow me to perform the duties of that position!"

"We will say no more about that," interrupted Tricolore, blushing.

"Certainly, madam. Well, you will doubtless remember that the Fairy Rancor was about to seize me. I had to be made to disappear, and my mother only succeeded in doing so by giving me the form of a tiny beast."

"That was very wise of her," observed the Princess; "there are far too many big beasts in the world."

"When I was a worm," continued Tactful, "I found I was the same all over; but as my love was inseparable from me, all my intelligence and all my sensations came together and lodged themselves in the place where you saw a kind of star."

"It is amazing what expression it gave to your face," said the Princess.

"Madam," exclaimed the Prince, "you surprise me, as I had no face; and to speak quite frankly to you, the star in question was on my tail."

"I know nothing about that," returned Tricolore; "but I repeat that you had a charming expression and that it was a lucky star."

"Indeed yes," agreed Prince Tactful. "I recollect that you took me gently in your fingers, that you squeezed me in a friendly way, and tickled me. I wriggled. You were apparently afraid of my escaping, so you pressed your thumb on me, and gave me the pleasure of killing me in the nicest way in the world."

"I assure you," declared Tricolore, "it had a great effect on me, and I felt . . ."

"You did not know," interrupted Tactful, "that in that moment I regained my human shape by your hand."

Chapter XIV

Beware of the Colic

The Princess remained for some moments pondering over the Prince's last observation, and a few tears even came into her eyes. Tactful was absorbed in gazing at Tricolore, and Tricolore was absorbed in meditation. Hence they preserved a selfish silence—the sure prelude to some important event. Tricolore broke this silence as follows:

"Who," she asked, "would have thought that the same moment which restored your freedom would give Potiron the right to become my husband?"

"If you wish it, madam," said the Prince circumspectly, "that could be remedied."

"And how?" asked Tricolore.

"Madam," replied the Prince, "in the

household of a Princess such as you are, there should be a large number of posts: Potiron's position is honorary, mine could be active."

"I fail to understand you," said Tricolore; "I want you to be my friend."

"How dear is that title to me!" exclaimed the Prince, and he pressed his lips to her hand.

The Princess did not withdraw it, but merely repeated weakly:

"Yes, you shall be my friend."

The Prince raised his head: he noticed that the color in Tricolore's cheeks had heightened and that her eyes had grown softer.

"How sweet is the sentiment you promise!" he continued. "How happy it will make me!"

"Do you think I am capable of it, then?" asked the Princess.

"Most certainly I do," replied Tactful. "Your eyes are full of friendship at this moment."

At the same time he tried to lean over the sofa on which she was lying.

"What are you doing?" she asked.

"Only giving you a proof of my friendship."

"You go too far!" she cried, in a voice into which she contrived to put displeasure.

I doubt, however, whether she was really displeased, for at that moment Potiron, who was attending the first levée, made a face, which the Fairy Slyness saw with delight.

"What is the matter with you, sir?"

"It is a sort of colic."

"You must be careful," said the Fairy. "Maladies of that kind often have evil effects."

120

But to return to Tricolore.

For a moment her attitude deceived Tactful; but, as he was a good reasoner, he soon saw that he must undertake to talk her into a reasonable frame of mind. And this is how he set about it:

"Might I make so bold as to ask you, madam, in what your idea of friendship consists?"

"To do everything in one's power," replied the Princess, "to please the object of it."

"But," demanded the Prince, "suppose that I were to ask you to travel a long way to do me a service?"

"I should leave immediately," replied the Princess earnestly.

"Madam," pursued Tactful, "I do not wish to put you to so much trouble. I only ask you to stay where you are."

"Let us change the subject," interrupted the Princess. "You do not know how to argue."

"Madam, allow me to ask you one more question. Imagine that Potiron has in his orchard a pomegranate tree: this tree bears only one pomegranate, which he has confided to your care; I am tolerably sure that no one would touch it; but let me pursue my reasoning. Imagine that there is a spell on this pomegranate, that it always remains the same and that one can remove a few seeds at a time without diminishing the total number, and without the fruit itself losing any of its freshness. Now your best friend comes to you, consumed with thirst, and in a feeble but tender voice says to you:

" 'Bountiful Princess, you see my condition, my body is consumed by a burning thirst, and is well-nigh exhausted;

122

one seed, one single seed from that delicious fruit would slake my soul and give me back my life; the master of the tree could not suffer any loss; he would not even notice that anything had occurred during his absence.'

"What would you do, Tricolore?"

Tricolore lowered her eyes, blushed, and seemed to seek for a reply, but without success.

"You say nothing," continued the Prince. "Ah! I believe you would let your friend die!"

The Princess, becoming more and more agitated, turned her head away and said:

"You are unbearable!"

In reply the Prince merely exclaimed:

"Ye gods! How thirsty I am!"

"Have done, I implore you!" Tricolore entreated in a voice which trembled when she tried to make it harsh. "Have done, sir!"

"But I tell you I am dying of thirst," he persisted, eagerly.

There was a short struggle, followed by a silence, which Tricolore interrupted by saying:

"Tactful! Dear Tactful!"

And at that moment Potiron, who was still with the King, threw himself on the floor crying:

"The colic! the colic! oh! I am dying!"

Chapter XV

A Remedy for the Colic

That particular moment was apparently a critical one for feminine virtue. The whole room was full of unfortunate husbands in contortions and grimacing; some were holding their stomachs, others, in spite of the respect due to the place they were in, had thrown themselves into arm-chairs. The Queen, who would have been charmed to give the colic to the King, came hurrying up to him:

"What is this all about?" she demanded.

The King, as usual, did not know what to say. The Fairy Rancor was raging inwardly with all her heart. The Fairy Slyness was laughing out loud with all hers.

The first attack came to an end. Calm was restored. All colic caused in the same manner has certain moments of respite. The Grand Instructor, on witnessing such strange occurrences, observed that one ought to render thanks to the gods for everything. Then he delivered a learned discourse upon the tricks of Fate. The King soon grew tired of listening to him, and remembered that it was the Council hour. Potiron went out with him. That day there was important business to be done. This had already been tabled and votes were about to be taken on the matter, when suddenly Potiron was seized with another violent attack of the colic; three-quarters of the Councilors were seized in the same way, and the floor of the Council Chamber was strewn with the forms of judges in convulsions, bumping into one another and shouting at the top of their voices. Potiron cried louder than any of them, and kept repeating alternately with the rest:

"Ah! my stomach! my stomach!"

Wigs and mortar-boards were strewn all over the place, for indeed the majority of the Councilors, though quite bald, were little more than wig-stands. The King sent for the Grand Instructor and for his Chief Physician. They entered the Council Chamber, preceded by the Queen and the Fairies. His Majesty gave an account of the seizure: the Doctor declared that it originated in the region of the liver; but the Fairy Slyness disconcerted him by saying:

"Lower down, Doctor, lower down!"

She admitted frankly that it was one of her usual tricks.

"I have wagered," she said, "that I

shall find out all the tricks which women play on their husbands, and I have cast a spell on them which gives a husband the colic every time he is tricked. It is just a little drawing-room joke of mine."

Potiron was dumb with rage; he fixed his gaze on his mother, the Fairy Rancor; and with a great effort he began to shout:

"Oh, Mother dear, I am—I am —But, madam," he went on, addressing the Fairy Slyness, "it is disgusting of you to have conceived such an idea. Do you mean to say that every time I have a stomach-ache—it will be a sure sign? . . ."

"A sure sign that your lady wife has not got one herself," finished the Fairy.

At this juncture Potiron made a face, and the Chief Physician said to him, feeling his pulse:

128

"My lord, you are grinding your teeth."

"Then one might wager," observed the Grand Instructor, "that the Princess must be making an altogether different use of hers."

"'Zounds!" cried Potiron. "I do not like this kind of joke; I know one certain remedy: I will go to my wife and lock her up; and as for her friend the Prince, I will—Oh, you vixen!" he cried, flinging himself on the ground. "Oh! What agony! Oh! Wretched woman! . . ."

"Quietly, my son, quietly," said the Fairy Rancor. "You must respect her sex."

"It appears to me," remarked the Queen, "that Prince Tactful has got the best of it."

Potiron was becoming more and more uneasy. He was bathed in perspiration.

The Chief Physician looked at his watch.

"What are you doing, Doctor?" cried poor Potiron.

"My lord," announced the Chief Physician, "I am just looking at my watch to find out how long the operation lasts."

This attack was much longer than the others.

"But, madam," observed the sufferer to the Fairy Slyness, "your son must be possessed of the Devil!"

"My lord," said the Fairy in a soft voice, "the Devil has always been kind enough to possess every member of my family. My son has the gift of being able to make colics of this kind last as long as he likes; that is why he is so popular at Court."

The King of the Patagonians then assumed a dignified air and expressed himself as follows:

"I think, nevertheless, that the time has come to put an end to this jest."

At that moment a far-away look came into the Grand Instructor's eyes, and he pronounced these holy words:

"The Divine Spirit inspires me: these colics will only cease when the Queen and the Princess have recovered their Maidenhood."

"They do not seem to be going about it very well," observed the Monarch.

"That means that I am quite incurable!" cried Potiron.

"No, my son, no, my dear child," interrupted the Fairy Rancor; "if it be only a question of the Maidenhood of the Queen and of the Princess, they will recover them. So much I will guarantee."

"You must have a marvelous gift for recovering things that are lost, Mother," said Potiron.

"In the gardens of the Palace," went on Rancor, "there is a fountain upon which I have cast a spell; its waters have the power of giving women back what they have lost, and girls what they ought to possess; but I warn you," she went on, "that the Queen and the Princess will only return to that state under very different conditions. The Queen will be compelled at last to pay her addresses to the King."

"I am deeply grateful," said the Monarch. "I am at last going to play an important part."

"As for you, my son," went on the Fairy, "if you want your colic to go, you will have to abandon this new treasure which your wife will enjoy, in favor of another."

"Why not?" retorted Potiron. "I am growing accustomed to doing so."

Chapter XVI

Pictures

Nothing is so tempting and so dangerous as a remedy which one does not
thoroughly understand. The enchanted
fountain should have been suspect,
since it was pointed out by a Fairy who
was never happy unless other people
were unhappy; but the results promised
by the fountain were very alluring.
Tricolore bathed in it and did well to do
so; the Queen followed her, and did ill.
The first recovered all the integrity of
a young maiden; but her mother fell into
a trap about which Rancor had been
very careful to say nothing. The fountain certainly possessed the marvelous
properties which she claimed for it; but
only for ladies who had never had more

than one lover. I do not include husbands: they do not count.

It produced quite a contrary effect on
women who had had more than one in-
trigue in their lives: the waters of the
fountain invariably developed on their
bodies the portraits of all their lovers,
and in order that there should be sufficient space they were all in miniature,
as though they had been painted to be
set in rings. The likenesses were striking, as the Queen found to her cost.
She plunged confidently into the fountain, but was astounded, on emerging,
to find herself so well adorned: she
recognized all her friends. She did her
utmost to wipe them from her body in
the same way as she had wiped them
from her heart, but the more she bathed
the brighter grew the colors: they were
all in proportion, the drawing was

accurate, and the coloring carefully
treated. They were so many master-
pieces of painting. The Queen, who
was no connoisseur, did not appreciate
the value of all this new talent. She
questioned her daughter, and was surprised that she did not wear the portrait
of the Grand Instructor; but as the Princess had received him from necessity,
no trace of him remained.

The spell only showed the portraits
of those to whom she had taken a fancy.
She was in this predicament when the
King was announced. This Monarch
was looking for her impatiently, and she
put up a resistance which, for the first
time in her life, was not feigned. A
wave of modesty swept over her face.
She recollected that her husband was
more curious than active, and his curiosity was, in the present case, all that

she dreaded. She hesitated and stammered, and the King thought she was being coy—a fact which redoubled his eagerness. He took her by the hand and drew her, despite a thousand excuses, into her apartment.

Arrived there her terror became extreme.

"Really, my lord," she said to him, "it seems to me that at our ages—it is hardly reasonable."

"What do you mean by ages, madam?" said the King. "The fountain has dispelled all that. You seem more beautiful, younger and fresher than on the day I married you: your Springtide has returned, and I think it has brought mine back with it."

And he became as importunate as any youngster.

"Really, my lord," protested the

Queen, repulsing him, "and in broad daylight too! . . ."

"What!" exclaimed the King. "What a marvelous woman! She is pretending to be modest! But I know quite well that she would be annoyed if I were to humor her!"

The Queen fell into a faint, and the King cried:

"Good heavens! Look at the portraits! But I know all those faces! There are all the young men of my Court: there are the Pages of my bedchamber; there is So-and-so, and So-and-so, and there is my son-in-law too; really they are speaking likenesses: it is the strangest sight I have ever set eyes on!"

The Queen recovered her senses and saw the King busily examining her through a magnifying glass.

"Your Majesty," said she, "must be very surprised."

"Extremely, madam, for you know how interested I am in Art. All these portraits are exquisite, and you would look admirable in a collector's cabinet. I think we shall have to send you to the Salon."

"Sire," said the Queen, "you must know how dear my friends are to me; I begged a Fairy to arrange for me to have all their portraits; but I did not expect her to place them there."

"I think it is very convenient," said the King. "It does not fill up one's pockets. But I am shocked at one thing about these portraits, and that is that I do not see mine amongst them, and I observe that all your friends are children between fifteen and twenty years of age at most."

"My lord," replied the Queen, "I am so afraid of losing them that I always choose them as young as I can."

"I have an idea," said the King suddenly. "I will have engravings made of all these portraits. The Grand Instructor is a very fine engraver. I will send for him at once."

Chapter XVII

Which is Too Much

In spite of the Queen's protests the Grand Instructor arrived. He took in the situation at a glance.

"This is something new in the way of a picture gallery!" he exclaimed. "What I like about it is that all these portraits can be moved so easily. It is what we scholars usually call a 'veni mecum'."

"They will make a fine set of engravings, at any rate," observed the King.

Then the Instructor asked the Queen:

"How do you want them engraved? Dry-point or etching?"

"Sir," snapped the Queen, "for Heaven's sake mind your own business!"

"It appears to me that a great many people have been minding yours!" retorted the Grand Instructor. "There is nothing I should like better than to do these engravings; but in all conscience it is not for the King to defray the cost of the plates."

"I understand you," admitted the King, "because I am a man of intelligence: those little friends look to me very much like so many lovers."

"I should think so, too," remarked the Grand Instructor. "This is a trick of the Fairy Rancor, who has decided that any portrait which ceases to be in the Queen's heart should pass to where you see it now."

The Fairy Rancor was sent for, and whilst awaiting her the Grand Instructor examined the portraits in detail with evident pleasure.

"Here are some beauties," he said; "they are only in pencil, but the poses

are delightful. They are real Clin-
chetels."

Rancor arrived.

"We are admiring your work," said
the King. "I must confess that this is
an extraordinary idea of yours."

"I wanted to find out," explained the
Fairy, "whether there was such a thing
as an irreproachable woman, and I conceived the idea of this enchanted fountain. If a single lady can be found," she
added, "who has not the smallest portrait on her body, all those of the Queen
will disappear."

"Then we must begin at once," cried
the Queen. "It will be all the easier because nearly every woman has bathed
in the fountain. All we have to do is to
line them up in the hall and to constitute
the Grand Instructor as Examiner."

"Madam," said he quickly, "it is in-

deed a right which I owe to my position,
but the decencies must be preserved,
and I insist on the examination being
made in my private house."

The suggestion was accepted: each
woman, without being told the reason,
was sent for and received according to
her rank. The Examiner acquitted himself of his task to the best of his ability.
He always began by saying: "Madam,
allow me to see if there is not something
beneath there."

This never failed. It was a perpetual
procession of women. The Queen
thought that the coquettes might break
the spell, but the holy Examiner observed that the only difference was in
the painting, and that the portraits of
their lovers were always in pastel. He
took it on himself to send them to Loriot
to have them fixed.

Amongst others sent for was a celebrated Holy Woman who hardly ever left the Temple near which she lived: she walked sedately, spoke dispassionately, and saw everything out of the corners of her eyes. She had, indeed, the most impressive reputation in the whole of the kingdom. The Grand Instructor observed that this woman was probably of no use for purposes of proof due to her immaculate existence.

"Virtue," said he, "rarely goes to the fountain—either from negligence, or because there is no need, or because she has no use for the privilege attached to it."

However, they took the risk. The Holy Woman was dumbfounded when the Examiner made her the following speech:

"Madam, in a moment your virtue is

about to be covered with the greatest glory. Allow me to do my duty."

"Insolence!" exclaimed the Holy Woman.

"It is my duty, madam."

"I will box your ears!"

"That is as may be."

Our female saint was furious. She beat, scratched, and bit him. The Examiner, however, full of enthusiasm, persevered in his task, and eventually triumphed.

"Oho!" he cried. "I am on my own ground here! Here are the portraits of all our good friends: I recognize all the novices and all the young monks attached to the Temple you attend. Here is the Procurer-General; here is the Rector, who is not called that for nothing, apparently. But really, madam, this is extremely edifying. Your body

146

looks like a congregation. But I see an
empty frame that spoils the effect; I will
soon put that right."

"Oh, my lord!" replied the Holy
Woman, covering her face with her
hands, "do not abuse your charge.
What are you doing? Will nothing
stop you? I shall never dare hold my
head up after this adventure—Ah, my
lord, you certainly have a great—gift for
painting!"

Thus it was that the Grand Instructor found himself heroically placed in
frame in his full robes. All the smaller
portraits had changed their positions
and seemed to be prostrated in respect
before his. The Grand Instructor had
this famous woman escorted honorably
back to her home, and judged this to be
a most convenient and proper moment
to end his task.

Prince Potiron, who was cured of his colic, resigned himself to Tricolore. All the Oracles, which seemed so contradictory, had come true. Prince Tactful had been the Princess's lover, but not her husband: which was all the better for her. Potiron had only possessed her like a fool and got no benefit out of it. So that he possessed her, yet did not possess her: she had come to him as a maiden and yet had had seventeen children. Tactful, by means of the enchanted fountain, had gathered her most precious flower, although in that he had been forestalled by the Grand Instructor. He had been killed by the hands of his mistress, and it was all the better for him. Potiron had had a violent attack of colic.

After such great adventures the two Fairies passed to other Courts. The

King went on vegetating in his own, and the Queen spent her time in adding to her collection of portraits.

END OF "ROYAL BED OF ROSES"

RHAPSODY RISQUE

RHAPSODY RISQUE

There would be none but happy people in this world, if only they always followed the laws of Nature and of Equity. There would be no harsh mothers, no deceitful daughters, no tedious husbands, no faithless wives.

Because life is conducted on quite different principles, the deceitful daughter one day becomes a suspicious and deluded mother, men and women buy instead of choosing one another, and marriage is made ugly by keeping it separate from love.

This moralizing is necessary for the justification of Zelmaide's character.

She was the daughter of a Queen (as you may well believe) who was called

the Rose Queen, in spite of the fact that
she was already old, and it was easy to
see from her hair that white was her
compulsory color—rose merely being
the color of her inclination.

She had once upon a time—that is to
say a long while since—married Prince
Gridelin, about whom I cannot discover
very much. We may presume that he
was no great warrior. His wife had,
quite rightly, become a widow. Zelmaide was her only daughter, and was
consequently very rich, and, as another
consequence, was destined to marry a
very stupid husband. He was a neigh-
boring Djinn, who was called the Stolid
Djinn, and who certainly lived up to his
name. He spoke little, thought even
less, and mooned a great deal. I have
never heard that he actually composed
anything, but had he done so it would

probably have been an ode in the fashion of the previous year.

At any rate, this was the husband
with whom Zelmaide was to be honored.
There was little to choose between their
circumstances, but their characters
were entirely different, so that the conditions were ideal for a modern marriage of convenience.

We may take it for granted that Zelmaide was a highly accomplished Princess; it only remains for me to attribute
a few faults to her, but I shall not avail
myself of the privilege, and so, to sum
her up in as few words as possible, I
may say that she was as charming as a
prude who prides herself on her re-
spectability.

The Rose Queen, whose skill did not
lay in the direction of bringing up children, had confided the Princess's edu-

cation to the Fairy Wisdom. This lady
was an aged and decrepit Fairy who,
they said, like all women of her age, had
once been as lovely as the day. Her
Palace was a long way from here: Tav-
ernier and Paul Lucas, who are inveter-
ate romancers, must have spoken about
it in their books of travel. At any rate
the novelists of the Palais-Royal, by dint
of traveling, on the map, along the
banks of the Escaut, the Lys and the
Rhine, have discovered that it was situated in Fairyland.

All children were sent to the Fairy
Wisdom. The great because it was the
thing to do, though it was a matter of
small consequence; the lowly on prin-
ciple, though it never did them any good.

The true art of the Fairy lay in pro-
ducing fairness of judgment and sound-
ness of heart, and in teaching children

to feel and to think, but at the same time she taught them to be moderate in their speech, to turn her lessons to account and to act upon her maxims. We may conclude from this that our modern historians, our story-tellers and, above all, I myself, were not educated by her. There were more scholars than wits in her Palace: no one felt flattered at being considered witty, and they were all convinced that it was easier to be a wit than a scholar.

As she had a large number of children under her care and was not a Fairy for nothing, she distinguished them by giving them each a magic taper, which had the gift of remaining alight so long as its owner followed out the Fairy's precepts, but which went out as soon as he or she wearied of them: in which case the owner had to leave the Palace. It is this

taper which was afterwards referred to
—at least, so I have been told—as the
Light of Reason.

The state of each taper told the Fairy
the tastes, inclinations and beliefs of her
disciples. The girls who were to become coquettes carried theirs in a dark
lantern; the budding prude lit hers as
soon as she saw any one coming, but
blew it out whenever she thought herself alone.

The philosophers' tapers were always
out, and yet they really believed that
theirs were burning brighter than those
of any one else. The Fairy would always send them home to their parents,
but this did not in any way lessen their
opinion of themselves. They mistook
pride for merit and argument for judgment. Poets, on the other hand, had
candles which burnt so brightly that

they were always guttering or burning right out in a single day.

For at least fifty years the Fairy had been unable to complete the education of any one of her pupils. The boys should have been sent for at the age of eighteen and the girls at sixteen, but she seldom managed to keep them even until they were seventeen and fifteen respectively: after that age their tapers were always going out: they always came to grief during the last year by the machinations of the Fairy Mischief, who was her mortal enemy.

Mischief was not one of those forbidding Fairies with serpents instead of hair, decayed teeth, eyes like live coals and chariots drawn by winged dragons. She was far more dangerous, for she was attractive instead of being repulsive, and she possessed the power of

appearing in any guise she wished to as-
sume; and she was careful always to appear quite charming in order to do harm
more surely and to be more skillfully
maleficent.

The Fairy Wisdom had no power to
keep her out of her Palace; her presence
was, in fact, a necessary ordeal for the
perfection of young people, though it
nearly always resulted in some unexpected imperfection.

To some she showed herself under
the guise of the Fairy Ambition, and
gave them a delightful picture of the
joys of power. It was useless for the
Fairy Wisdom to try to paint these
joys in their true colors, that is to say,
very somber ones; the pupils listened
politely but incredulously; the picture
drawn by the Fairy Mischief flattered
their vanity, and that was quite suffi-

cient; the pride of those to whom she spoke already appropriated to itself the deference due to rank, and the breath of vanity extinguished their tapers.

Mischief carefully studied the moral characters of all the girls; on those who had none (as frequently occurred) she impressed the delight and glory of attracting a score of lovers without loving any of them, calling the art of catching them, intelligence, shrewdness in keeping them amused, kind-heartedness, and the pleasure of laughing at them, good manners.

If by any chance she found any who were really kind-hearted, she made dupes of them, inspiring them with the desire for love and praising the delights of constancy and of true love. It was in vain that the Fairy Wisdom, who, though virtuous, was no prude, and

who was charming without hypocrisy,
pointed out to them that such happiness
depends too much on the person upon
whom one settles one's affections: they
did not believe her. Their pride, that
stupid pride which is capable of shaping
so many virtues and which yet ruins
nearly all of them, persuaded them that
the Fairy was mistaken, and that it was
not possible for any one ever to stop loving them.

The Fairy Mischief concentrated all
her efforts on Zelmaide, even neglecting
to lead the other pupils astray, and the
Fairy Wisdom made the best of the opportunity by completing the education
of two or three boys, who could never
afterwards find any employment in the
world because they were considered
too peculiar, and of a couple of girls,
who were wisely compelled to take the

veil in order to try to make them mend their ways.

Zelmaïde was fifteen years old, and until that time her little taper had always shone as brightly as a votive candle. But there chanced to be a certain young man named Zulmis there, and he it was who prevented it from burning until the end. He was the son of the King of Cochin China. He was a nice little fellow who spoke Spanish like an Indian, English like a Turk, and French like Richardson's Pamela.

He created fashions, possessed a Baillon watch, was clever at inventing riddles, and knew the Bal de Strasbourg by heart. He had given orders for the Lyons coach to bring him any new books of interest, a middle-class comedy transcribed by Minet, and the ribbon of the order of St. Michael; but all these things were confiscated at a frontier post of the realm of the Fairy Wisdom. Although he was quite happy by himself, he nevertheless liked the company of Zelmaide, whom he saw occasionally, and who found it quite as amusing to listen to him as to read the Mercury.

The Fairy Mischief, in order to confirm him in his growing interest in this young Princess, often assumed the appearance of the Fairy Wisdom and praised the qualities of Zulmis to her. The Princess adored the Fairy on these occasions, and never found so much sense in her as when she was entirely lacking in it; when next she saw the Fairy Wisdom she would bring the conversation back to Zulmis, and the Fairy would tell her to be careful of him. The Princess could not reconcile these contradictory moods, and ended by saying that the Fairy Wisdom was becoming old and feeble-minded.

One day when she was strolling in a little thicket near the Palace, she came across Zulmis deep in thought; in her agitation she could not help disturbing him. The Fairy Mischief had managed to stage this chance encounter, for by helping them she hoped to deceive others, and was preparing, perhaps, to deceive them too one day.

"I thought I was alone here," exclaimed Zelmaide in confusion, still grasping her candle, which she was beginning to find rather a nuisance.

"I never thought I should meet you here either," said Zulmis; "I was quite content with dreaming of you; but since chance has thrown us together, and since we are both pupils of the Fairy Wisdom, let us see, by reasoning together, if we have derived any profit from her lessons."

"Gladly," cried Zelmaide, "for I love an argument. You have just told me that you were dreaming of me; what were you dreaming about me? I am curious to know whether your dreams of me resemble in any manner my dreams of you."

"What!" cried Zulmis, "you dream about me, Zelmaide?"

"Of course," she answered, with a frankness that explained why her candle was still alight; "but I only do so at night, because the Fairy Wisdom has forbidden me to think of you by day."

"Ah! for my part," said the Prince, "every hour, every moment, sleeping or waking, you are the one object of my dreams and of my thoughts. You excite feelings in me which I do not under-

stand: a turmoil of imaginings and emotions which torment me and yet give me
happiness. I try to analyze them, but I
cannot do so; but one thing I understand even less, and that is that my mind
and my heart, which are, I am assured
by the Fairy, entirely independent of my
body, seem inevitably to react upon it at
such moments, and each one of their
emotions seems to be reflected in it. Yes,
my adorable Zelmaide, as soon as I begin to think of you, as soon as I begin to
dream of you, I leave my natural state,
but only to pass into another which is a
thousand times preferable. In fact, at
the moment when you appeared I was
enjoying all its delights . . ."

"Why, to be sure," said Zelmaide,
"your eyes seem to be quite changed;
but please do not let that trouble you:
I like them just as much as they are."

"Can it be, Zelmaide, that your condition in any way resembles mine?"

"Well—" she replied, "yes—perhaps —that is to say, I cannot be quite sure. Since we are discussing the question, I will try to describe my feelings to you. I dream about you more than I think about you, but that is apparently out of respect for the Fairy's wishes. When I am awake I do not look for you, but I am always hoping to find you. Your conversation pleases me: it amuses me without making me laugh, and I like that because it does not make me appear frivolous. You are perhaps no more intelligent than other young men, and yet the things you say to me please me more: doubtless it is the way in which you say them. When you leave me I grow sad: it is as though you took my happiness away with you, leaving me in a state of languor of which I am ashamed without knowing why. That is how my days are passed."

"And your nights?" asked Zulmis, gazing tenderly at her.

"Ah, Zulmis! those I dare not describe to you!"

"But why? Who is to prevent you?" pleaded Zulmis, kissing her hand. "Are you afraid of making me too happy? Please tell me."

"Oh, be careful!" cried the Princess, "you will make me drop my taper! I have already had several anxious moments with it through you."

"In what way?" asked Zulmis.

"Do you want me to tell you everything?" protested Zelmaide. "Really, Zulmis, I am beginning to lose all patience with you."

"It would grieve me greatly to offend

you," urged the Prince, "but I am
racked with curiosity."

"Very well, then," said she, "I will
satisfy it for you. You know that the
chief thing the Fairy Wisdom enjoins
on all her maidens is always to keep
their tapers alight: on that entirely de-
pend, according to her, their reputation,
their virtue, and their future marriage.
The essential matter, so she says, is
never to have any predilection for any
but the man one marries. If, unfortunately, one shows a preference for any
one else, good-by taper, out it goes, and
one's honor vanishes with its flame."

"Yours," said Zulmis, "burns very
brightly; I cannot believe that it has ever
been in any danger."

"Well—yes," Zelmaide hesitated, "it
is quite true that it is burning; and
yet it seems to give less light than when

I met you. I am rather anxious about it."

"Why, when you have no cause for anxiety?" asked Zulmis. "But we seem to be straying from the most interesting point in our conversation."

"I am afraid I have forgotten what it was," confessed Zelmaide. "What were we talking about?"

"About your nights," answered Zulmis.

"True, I remember now," said Zelmaide. "Really, Zulmis, I think it is wrong of me to confide these things to you. And yet they are only dreams, and as you are the object of them you may as well be the confidant of them too."

"Ah! Now you are becoming reasonable!" cried Zulmis.

"I wonder!" mused Zelmaide. "My taper is spluttering terribly; just as though a drop of water had got into it."

"Let us return to your dreams, I implore you!" begged Zulmis.

"Well, then, my dreams—I do not understand them. The Fairy has often told me that dreams are nothing but impressions made on our minds by the thoughts that have occupied us in the daytime. But mine are not like that, because they throw me into a state of disorder and delight which I never feel, and of which I never have the least inkling, all the time I am awake. You have often been told that I was destined to marry the Stolid Djinn; I have only seen him when he came here twice with my mother: I am told that he thought me pretty; I don't know whether any one told him that I thought him very stupid."

"That shows," interrupted Zulmis,

"that you both have a very nice judgment."

"I was always being told," continued Zelmaide, "that he was to be my husband. I asked the Fairy what a husband was; she answered that he was some one whom one had to love with all one's heart. This troubled me, for I should have liked him, since one has to love one's husband, to have been fashioned so as to make love a pleasure rather than a precept. The Fairy would then say that one must not discuss things of this sort. This is one of the things that irritate me most about the Fairy Wisdom. She seems only to employ argument in order to exclude discussion. I always left these conversations in a far from satisfactory state of mind.

"One day you and I met by chance,

and we had a conversation which seemed to improve our acquaintance with each other. This acquaintance soon ripened, and we became friends. You fulfilled the idea I had formed of what a husband should be; I spoke about it to the Fairy, who scolded me and warned me that my taper would be extinguished for ever if I had any inclination for any one but the Stolid Djinn.

"This talk put me in a bad temper, and I retired to bed early. I had hardly fallen asleep when I imagined myself to be awakened; I saw you come into my room, and you never seemed so much the ideal of a husband as you were then. Your hair was ruffled and your sparkling eyes seemed to hold none but melting looks. You threw yourself at my feet—you kissed my hand, which I tried to hide from you—you tried to find

it again, and I was glad you did so—
Ah, Zulmis! I dare not go on. I am
certainly committing a fault in telling
you all this: I am blushing, and one
never blushes unless one is doing
wrong."

"Then I am doing wrong in listening
to you," said Zulmis in a troubled voice,
"for I too feel the color rising to my
cheeks; yet it does not worry me. Go
on, sweet Zelmaide, and make my happiness complete."

"I cannot summon up the strength to
refuse," confessed the Princess. (The
reader must know that at this point
the flame of Zelmaide's candle grew
much dimmer without her noticing it.)
"Where was I?" she continued. "I am
always losing the thread of my story and
having to appeal to you."

"And yet I do not interrupt you," replied Zulmis. "You were talking, I think, about your hand, which you were glad I was trying to find. It only remains to know whether I was fortunate enough to do so."

"Oh, yes!" continued the Princess, "I was hiding it, I remember, because you were disturbing my serenity too much —but it did not do me much good (which proves that nothing is wholly evil). I do not know how it happened, but in my determination to refuse you that liberty I allowed you others of which I never dreamt, and against which I could not therefore guard myself. You became more insistent and I became more disturbed. It was in vain that I resisted you, and in vain that I cried out that I detested you: apparently my expression belied my words; however, I summoned all my strength to mark my anger against you, when suddenly I caught sight of the Fairy Wisdom. The sight of her terrified me, but the sweetness of her expression calmed me down again. It is much nicer to see her in a dream than in one's waking hours.

" 'Why, Zelmaide,' she asked me, 'do you resist this Prince so much? He loves you, he attracts you; so that he must be the man whom the gods have destined to be your husband. It would be unjust of them to give you any other and to command you to have feelings other than those with which they inspire you.' "

"Indeed, I agree with you," exclaimed Zulmis. "The Fairy reasons much better at night than in the daytime. Well, and what answer did you give her?"

"Alas, Zulmis! I did not answer her; I sighed, I looked at you, I felt your arms about me—I lost sight of the Fairy. I wanted to call to her, but I could only pronounce these words: 'Ah, Zulmis!—My dear Zulmis! What are you doing?' And then I found myself in a state of agitation which I cannot describe to you.

"I awoke, and thought myself lost; I hurriedly glanced at my taper, and was quite surprised to see that it was burning even more brightly than when I had gone to bed."

"There can be no doubt at all, Zelmaide," exclaimed Zulmis, "but that this dream was a command from the gods. My whole heart tells me that it must be so: never have I felt so much piety. Yes, your story has lifted me out of myself; doubtless, it is because I am animated by

a divine flame—and I read in your eyes
that you also feel its influence! Ah, I
am so happy."

"Zulmis! Zulmis!" cried the Princess. "Can I believe this to be true,
when my mother's plans are so much
opposed to it? It seems to me that our
mothers should only desire what the
gods ordain, or that the gods deceive
us in making us yearn for what our
mothers forbid."

(At this point certain critics might
perhaps imagine that I have been crib-
bing from the Pastor Fido, but they
would be mistaken: I have only copied
his methods of argument.)

This fine reasoning did not discon-
cert the Prince, who began to impor-
tune Zelmaide as though she were still
dreaming. She took to flight; but she
met the Fairy Mischief who, in the guise

of the Fairy Wisdom, stopped her, and
gave Zulmis time to catch her, disap-
pearing at the same moment. This
sight redoubled the insistence of the
Prince. Zelmaide still struggled to escape from him; but suddenly her taper
slipped from her hand, and went out as
it fell.

"Ah! I am undone!" she cried. "All
my fears are realized! Wretch! It is
your fault that my taper has gone out: I
shall never dare show myself again to
the Fairy."

"Well, then, let us get out of her
sight," suggested Zulmis; "cannot we be
happy without her?"

At this Zelmaide burst into tears.

"Alas! You will desert me! I cannot
trust myself to you—No, I must find my
taper again."

And she stooped down to grope for it.

But she stumbled, and fell into the arms of Zulmis.

"Ah, Zulmis!" she cried. "You are betraying me! It is dreadful of you—Zulmis!—Zulmis!—Will you have done?

"Ah!—I hate you!—I will never forgive you—Yes, I am sure you will be faithless to me!"

Zulmis overwhelmed her with kisses, without paying any heed to her protestations.

"What!" he exclaimed at last, his voice shaking with happiness. "Are all these charms to become the prey of the Stolid Djinn? Zelmaide! Adorable Zelmaide! . . ."

At this point speech abandoned them both, and their conversation consisted of silence and kisses, followed by kisses and silence. Zelmaide recovered herself and tried to say, "I abhor you!" But her voice faltered, and with a sigh she whispered: "Ah, Zulmis! I adore you!"

The reader hardly, I imagine, expects that Zelmaide should recover her taper: indeed, she did not even trouble to look for it; but when she recovered from her intoxication, and when she could consider calmly the victory which Zulmis had won, her soul was filled with shame and remorse. One never feels so modest as when one has just been discarding modesty. She reproached the Prince bitterly, and knew she would never dare appear again before the Fairy. In fact, it was the Fairy Mischief herself who, proud of her handiwork, hastened to tell the Fairy Wisdom all about it. However, Zulmis was so persuasive that he dispelled all Zelmaide's fears. Thereupon they left this irrational Palace together. I do not know

whether they were as pleased as I am to
have left this Palace of Reason: I was
afraid of never escaping from it, and I
do not think they will ever get me back
there.

So off they went on their travels, having gained love and lost reason: they did
not travel very far, because pleasure
made them halt so often. But pleasure
is an obstacle which soon wears down.
Zulmis, after several active proofs of his
opinions, was reduced to merely assur-
ing her of them. He swore to Zelmaide
that he would always love her, and began to make pretty speeches to her. But
Zelmaide had not yet learnt that protestations of love are only a makeshift, and
that it is only deeds that really prove
one's vows. One day in a wood (for
these things must always happen in a
wood) they came upon a Tortoise,

which told them in a drawling voice that it was a Fairy, that it knew them, and that it was protecting them. Its way of drawing out its sentences over a quarter of an hour so delighted our lovers that they adopted it themselves: they even made it the fashion at Court for a short time. But as all art degenerates when it becomes perfect, nowadays it is no longer words that drag, but thoughts.

Zelmaide was a little worried at hearing that the Tortoise knew her; however, she grew accustomed to it.

"I know that you are weary," this Fairy told them, "and I have crawled here especially to put my carriage at your disposal."

And indeed there was a chariot drawn by six tortoises standing nearby. The Prince and Princess sat themselves in it, and the Tortoise, their protectress,

let them drive off in it. It will easily be
guessed that it was the Fairy Mischief
who had assumed this shape; nor was it
the last that she was to take.

The slow progress of the carriage
fretted Zulmis a great deal and gave Zelmaide the megrims; they began, through
their yawns, to assure each other of how
happy they were. Their conversation
became imperceptibly monosyllabic.
The Prince fell asleep, which shocked
the Princess, and bitterness began to
mingle with her feelings. Then the
Prince left the carriage for a moment,
and the six tortoises became six butter-
flies which carried Zelmaide off to the
Fairy Coquette.

Zulmis was very astonished when she
disappeared from view, and he felt terribly ashamed of finding himself on foot
like a traveling mountebank; in fact, the

only person who appeared more foolish
than he was the Stolid Djinn, who had
arrived at the Fairy Wisdom's Palace
with the Rose Queen to come to fetch
Zelmaide to marry her. He was dumbfounded when he heard that she was no
longer in the Palace. The Queen, who
had left it at the age of fourteen in much
the same way, made a great scene, but
secretly admired the patience and virtue
of her daughter; nor is she the only one
who has thought the same in similar circumstances. The Djinn did not listen
to a word of what was being said, but
replied to everything. His face was the
mirror of his soul; he had small features
hidden amongst folds of puffy flesh; in
fact he looked like a baby seen through
a magnifying glass. He had a brother
whose mind was even inferior, and who
was called the Stupid Djinn, to distin-

guish him. In spite of this they were often taken for one another.

His fury knew no bounds, and he kept on saying: "I cannot understand reasons"—which was indeed the case. "I want my wife. I have been counting on her; if you take me for a fool you are making a great mistake; in short, I don't want to be made a fool of. If the Princess has been given to another, I want her back; and if it is she who has given herself to another, she must be sent back to her mother and put into the Bridewell."

To calm him they told him that his reasoning was excellent, and they undertook to make inquiries as to what had happened to Zelmaide. This succeeded in quieting the Djinn. In fact, he went away with the Queen, and, as he was a very astute young man, he

asked every traveler he met, in an off-
hand manner, whether they had, per-
chance, noticed a young woman who
was being quite voluntarily taken away
by a young fop. If by any chance one
of them had come across a man and a
woman, he informed the Djinn.

"Ah! then," he would ask eagerly;
"was not this woman or girl named Zelmaide?"

"I do not know her name," would be
the reply.

"Then how the devil do you expect
me to recognize her?" he would say.
Then he would preen himself and say to
the Queen: "One has to be cunning; the
first thing to ask is a person's name. It
is a much more certain way of recogniz-
ing people than by their features."

The journey was spent in this kind of
conversation, a fact which made the

Queen very glad that her daughter had escaped. She was, however, always tactful with the Stolid Djinn, as she could not hope to give her daughter another husband without his consent. Such was the decree of Fate: for one can no more avoid Fate in a Fairy Story than one can avoid tambourines and pantomime in a modern opera.

But I must return to Zelmaide, who had reached the Palace of the Fairy Coquette, and I shall let Zulmis continue walking for some time before recounting his adventures.

The Princess was not at all happy in this new Palace. She possessed too much intelligence to be amused by women who often debased theirs into pantomime, and she had made too good a beginning with Zulmis to be satisfied with a country in which love and temperament were only mental emotions.

She saw several maidens there who had failed to get married, even though they really were maidens; but appearances had been against them, and in these matters appearances count much more than reality.

She also saw several women who were separated from their husbands, but who had nothing with which to reproach themselves but frivolousness; their husbands were not to blame because, their dishonor being merely a matter of prejudice, their wives' sin consisted more in flouting public opinion than in infidelity.

The Rose Queen, who knew her own flesh and blood, had a very good idea of the road taken by Zelmaide. She herself, in spite of her age, often made the same journey: she had been a coquette in her youth, and was still a coquette in her old age; for it is a folly which always survives the qualities which make it bearable: we like it when it is merely a fault, but we scoff at it when it becomes ridiculous.

She put on her rose-colored scarf, her green-flowered dress, and her white shoes embroidered with silver. Nor did she neglect to put on a double layer of rouge. She placed her patches tastefully, examined herself in her mirror, simpered, and started off.

All the gates of the Palace were open: nothing flatters the empire of coquetry so much as the homage and aspirations of an old woman. She discovered her daughter, terrified her by her presence, and reassured her by her caresses.

"Come and embrace me, my poor Zelmaide!" she cried; "come, do not be afraid of your mother; we are together now, and you know that I only visited the Fairy Wisdom in order to take you away. Confide in me: did you come here because you wanted to, or because you were bored?"

"Alas, Mamma!" replied Zelmaide, "I am so wretched!"

"And what are you wretched about?" asked the Queen, kindly. "Tell me all your faults, my dear girl, and I will forgive you them with as much indulgence as if I had never committed any myself."

"You reassure me, Great Queen," sighed Zelmaide. With these words she passed her hand across her brow, summoned all her wits and, after a moment's silence, expressed herself as follows: "Ah, Mamma, what a long time it is to wait until I am sixteen before getting married!"

"Now I understand," remarked the Queen; "I felt just like you do at your age. When I was fourteen I began to find the evenings at the Fairy Wisdom's Palace very long: so I discovered the secret of shortening them. I used to go out, like you; I trusted myself to a coxcomb who deceived me. I was promised in marriage to Prince Gridelin. I had to have recourse to a ruse in order to hoodwink him. I retired, under pretext of piety, to a Community of Virgins dedicated to the Goddess Isis. Prince Gridelin was informed of this, and thought I had only left the Palace of the Fairy Wisdom in a fit of religious fervor. This merely increased his love, so that he came to see me several times, and became very insistent, though I always resisted him. I yielded in the end, when my part was played, and from that moment I have always been happy and respected."

"Ah, madam!" cried Zelmaide. "The story you have just told me is my own."

"I thought so," said the Queen. "You have listened to the persuasions of some young man: which proves your sincerity. You granted him favors: which shows your kindness of heart. And now you want to recover your reputation and deceive a husband: which shows your intelligence."

"I would gladly remain unmarried," explained Zelmaide, "under the conditions of the last year. But I imagine that as one grows older one loses the respect of other people, which is the payment one has to make for pleasure. So I will do the same as you did. Take me, pray, to this Community of Virgins."

"Certainly, my child," said the Queen;

"but I must warn you of a circumstance that may prove rather embarrassing: no doubt you were rather weak with this young lover, whose name you have not told me?"

"His name is Zulmis," replied Zelmaide, "and he is a Prince and a very gallant man."

"Then he has deceived you," the Queen assured her; "for these gentlemen are much less scrupulous on the question of love than they are on that of glory.

"But to come back to the embarrassing circumstance. You must leave this House of Isis by a different gate from the one by which you enter, and it is called the Gate of Ordeal. You are led through it by your future husband: he can, if he likes, take you away by the entrance gate, but if he is a little uncer-

tain about you—as is frequently the case
—he always insists upon the other. If
a girl has retired into this Temple in a
fit of religious fervor, she passes out un-
molested; if, however, her conduct has
not been irreproachable, the door bangs
to and she cannot get out, but is con-
demned to remain in that House of Pen-
ance for the rest of her life."

"Oh, Mother!" cried Zelmaide, "that
is an embarrassing circumstance. How
did you manage to get through it?"

"Prince Gridelin was so convinced of
my chastity," replied the Queen, "that
he would have thought it an insult to
make me pass through the Gate of Ordeal; but it is rare to find men who are
so credulous. The Stolid Djinn is too
stupid not to be suspicious."

"Never mind," said Zelmaide, "it is
my only chance, and I must risk it. How-

ever, I will confess to you that I love
Zulmis more than ever: I am anxious
about him; the thought of the dissipa-
tions of the world does not soothe my
anxiety, and it will only increase if I try
to calm it.

"If Zulmis is lost to me, I will cheerfully consent to spend my life in the
Community of Virgins. Should absence
make him reflect on his ingratitude,
should repentance bring him back,
should he try to find me again, his love
will return in greater measure than before when he discovers that, when I left
him, I fled from all other men to dream
of him from the depths of solitude."

The Queen, who was as delighted as
she was surprised at having given birth
to a sentimental child, took her to the
Temple of Isis without any further delay. She sent for the High Priestess and

introduced Zelmaide to her as a model
of propriety. The Priestess looked at
her kindly, and replied in honeyed ac-
cents that it was not at all surprising,
considering whose daughter she was.

"I shall be delighted to have her,
Great Queen," she went on, "but as a
matter of form I must ask our Moderator. I have no doubt that he will ap-
prove of the admission of the Princess;
permit me to send for him."

A few moments later the Moderator
entered: he was a High Priest of Isis, a
remarkably handsome man, about six
feet in height, with brown eyebrows and
clean-cut features; from his expression
one gathered that the Gate of Ordeal
was not for him.

"I want you to look carefully," said
the Priestess to the Queen, "at the venerable Shaft of Light from the Holy God-

dess. He sheds his blessings on our House; never have we had so many Virgins as since we have been fortunate enough to have him in our midst."

"I can well believe it," replied the Queen; "in my time you only had an ugly little priest whom we all detested."

"I remember him," said the Priestess. "He was sent to us by the Goddess in a fit of temper. Well, most venerable sir," she went on, "what do you think of the Princess?"

"I think," he answered, "that she is quite likely to attract to us the heavenly influences of the Goddess, and, unless I am mistaken, it is virtue that brings her, just as it is virtue that keeps me, here."

"You are very polite," murmured Zelmaide, in confusion.

"Oh! Our Venerable Moderator is a great connoisseur," observed the Priestess. "You will learn that by experience."

After this interchange of compliments, the Queen left the Princess in the care of the Priestess and the Moderator and returned to her Palace, with the object of acquainting the Stolid Djinn of her daughter's excessive zeal.

We will now leave the Princess for a moment to follow the adventures of Zulmis.

The departure of Zelmaide revived his passion for her; he roused himself, prayed to the Goddess of Love, and even appealed to the Tortoise Fairy. He lifted up his voice against the gods and against destiny. Indeed, this was the first monologue ever made: it often happens that the people who indulge in them nowadays fail to be grateful to him to whom this invention is due; he did not,

however, pace to and fro, but kept
straight on his way; at last exhaustion
came to his rescue, and he lay down and
went to sleep. . . .

The reader quite understands that I
cannot possibly pass by such a fine opportunity for putting in a dream. Indeed, an hour after he had fallen asleep,
just as dawn was about to break, when
all dreams are true, he imagined that he
was wafted into a palace which was ob-
viously a very magnificent one; it was
inhabited by two fairies. The task of
one of them was to collect quantities of
particles of a subtle and spiritual substance, and with them to make human
minds. These minds all differed from
one another: fine or poor, quick or slow,
solid or superficial, gentle or caustic,
according to the substance of which they
were made: for often a certain amount

of coarse material got mixed with them,
as a result of which they became heavy;
and oftener still specks of saltpeter,
which gave a satirical and cruel turn to
the mind. In short, the characters of the
different minds depended upon the in-
gredients of the mixture, and became
noble and spirited or base and cringing,
in accordance. Vices and virtues were
introduced into the substance compos-
ing each mind, and developed at the
same time as the organs of the bodies
which they were to animate.

When the Fairy had made a certain
number of minds, she handed them over
to the other Fairy, whose name was the
Fairy Malice, and whose task was to
make bodies out of solid matter. Since
she was malicious and frequently mischievous, she amused herself by making
all the figures different from each other.

After applying herself seriously to making a well-made man, she grew weary of the effort, and jestingly made a dozen other bodies all hunchbacked or twisted. She treated faces in the same way: after making a dozen handsome ones, she would make thirty which were quite ridiculous: some squinted, others had flattened noses, some, though nearly perfect, lacked all animation, whilst others looked coarsely bred. Such was the Fairy's capriciousness that she was even more ingenious in the pranks she played upon women: she seemed often to be actuated by the very best motives in the world in giving some of them every bodily perfection, only to give them the most abominably ugly heads. At other times she would fashion bodies offending against every standard of gracefulness, waistless and with neither curves nor softness, but would give them charming faces; the fate of the first was to give a great deal of pleasure to any lover they might have, and of the second to be much sought after.

But all this was only the Fairy's more innocent mischief. Unfortunately she had the right to animate each of these bodies with whatever mind she cared to choose. And as she was fully aware of the condition and career which destiny had allotted to each of them, the mind that she imprisoned in each body was nearly always the opposite to the one it should have had.

Such a novel spectacle inspired Zulmis with curiosity to discover what kind of mind animated Zelmaide. He asked the Fairy Malice, who replied as follows:

"Zelmaide is a perfect Princess, and I

had not a single evil intention in shaping her, from head to foot, a thing which has not happened to me for a long time; but I gave her too sensitive a soul, and I am very sorry I did so, for she has conceived a mad infatuation for a certain Zulmis, who is charming enough, but is a bit of a coxcomb; so, as a punishment, he will see this Princess again, but she will treat him like a dog, and he will spend thirty nights with other beautiful ladies without deriving any benefit from them."

This prophecy made him so unhappy that he awoke; he found himself alone in the damp grass, and he felt even more weary from the journey he had made than frightened by his dream. However, he started off again without any definite object in view, being just as perturbed about the treatment he was to receive

from the Princess as about the treatment he was to mete out to the other
beauties. Fatuously, he imagined—for
vanity always sees everything in relation
to itself—that they were thirty tests to
which Zelmaide would put him, and
thirty sacrifices that he would make to
her.

He was proceeding in this assurance
when he found himself in a broad avenue leading to a castle: he hoped that he
might find Zelmaide there; so his chief
motive in following the avenue was love,
although he had a more urgent one,
which was hunger and fatigue. At the
gate barring the first courtyard he found
two dwarfs pretending to be giants; he
asked them politely if Princess Zelmaide
were not in the Palace. They replied
disdainfully that they knew nothing
about that.

"At least, gentlemen," he pursued with even more humility, "will you be good enough to tell me the name of your master or of your mistress?"

"I Don't Know What," they replied together, raising their voices.

"Ah, gentlemen!" begged Zulmis, "have compassion on a poor Prince who is only asking you the name of . . ."

"Devil take it!" cried one of the dwarfs, interrupting him; "we are tired of telling you that the Palace belongs to Fairy I Don't Know What."

"Oh, I beg your pardons!" said Zulmis. "You mean that the name of your mistress is I Don't Know What?"

"Yes, my boy," answered the other dwarf; "don't you understand plain speech?"

Whilst this conversation was going on, the Fairy I Don't Know What returned from taking the air, and asked the dwarfs who the man at the door was. They replied that it was Prince I Don't Know Who. Zulmis approached the Fairy with dignity, bowed slightly to her, and paid her a neat compliment. This beginning accorded well with the Fairy's character, and gave her a good opinion of the qualities of Zulmis. She bade him accompany her, and whilst crossing the courtyard on the way to her apartments she questioned him, interrupted him, praised him, and contradicted him. The Prince was quite at a loss, and saw how the Fairy had come by her name, which was quite in accordance with her intellect and even with her appearance, for she was quite different to other people: she had fair hair and dark skin, one large handsome eye, one small pretty one, and her other features were in keeping. She

had flaccid cheeks because they ought
to have been firm, and a hard character
because it ought to have been gentle. So
far that was all the Prince knew about
her.

The Fairy ordered dinner, which
pleased Zulmis extremely; but when it
was announced she declared that she
was not feeling well and would not eat
until that evening, and this annoyed
Zulmis extremely.

She was as temperamental as she was
bad tempered, which was a great trial to
her, and sometimes even made her oblig-
ing in spite of herself; but she was very
hard to please, and even in the throes of
enjoyment always managed to discover
circumstances which might afford her
an opportunity for anger.

She did not know Zulmis yet, and, so
that he should not know her too well, she

told him that she was very seriously
minded. When he started a discussion
she yawned: he turned the conversation
to sentiment and she scoffed at him; he
became playful and she took offense.
The Prince was entirely nonplussed.
Finding it too hot in her apartment, she
went out into the garden. As soon as she
got there she said it was too damp and
went in again, still accompanied by Zulmis, who by this time had no further
need to ask what her name was.

At last supper-time came: she entered
the dining-room, where she sat opposite
to the Prince with her elbows on the
table. She abused everything in an
undertone, found fault with all the
dishes, hustled the servants, and paid
the Prince compliments in such a half-
hearted and off-hand way that it
seemed as though she were reproach-

ing him for something. He made all the
wrong replies, because he could not
understand the questions; besides
which, of course, he ate a great deal,
which made him appear a boor.

After supper she asked him if he could
read Comedies.

"No, madam," he replied, "I have
neglected that study, because I was told
that the art was a lost one."

"That is a fatuous remark," the Fairy
told him; "where were you educated?
At least you play some game?"

"I only know backgammon, madam."

"That's a pretty choice!" was her sour
comment. "You must have been an
Oratorian Father!"

"Madam," he corrected her humbly,
"I am only a Prince."

"My poor friend," she retorted, "you
seem very delicate for such a calling."

"Madam," said Zulmis, "if it would amuse you, I will tell you my story."

"No, indeed," said she hastily. "I would as soon read the story of the Mangy Wolf. I really think the best place for you is bed; besides, it is getting late."

Whereupon the Prince respectfully took his leave of the Fairy, and asked one of her women where he should sleep. The woman burst out laughing in his face, and told him that there was but one bed in the house, and that was the Fairy's; that sometimes she made strangers sleep in the courtyard, but that when she had done them the honor of allowing them to dine with her, she usually gave them the pleasure of sleeping in it. So saying, she led the Prince into the Fairy's apartment. The Fairy had already let down her hair and removed her rouge, but this did not rouse Zulmis at all.

"I believe," she told him, "that you were stupid enough to think that I had several beds in this Palace; I have reduced everything to simple necessaries, and since two people can sleep together it is obvious that of two beds one is superfluous. We should be economical and hospitable. I fulfill the first condition by not multiplying useless furniture, and I acquit myself of the second by allowing you to sleep with me."

With this all the maids left the room, and the Prince found himself alone with the Fairy.

"Madam," he began, falteringly. "Really—I am very—very sensible of . . ."

"That is not what I ask of you," interrupted the Fairy; "all that I insist

upon is that you should be grateful;
nothing more, nothing less."

"Great Fairy!" confessed Zulmis,
plucking up courage. "I would most
gladly accept your favors, but to tell you
the truth my affections are already
pledged."

"Pledged?" asked the Fairy. "Tell
me, please, what you mean by 'pledged'?
This is something new to me."

"Can it be possible?" exclaimed Zulmis. "Can you really be ignorant of an
effect of which you must so often have
been the cause?"

"Well," replied the Fairy, "what you
say may be very nice, though I do not
pretend to understand it; but I am in
mortal fear lest it should really prove to
be rather insipid. To come back to my
question. I understand, then, that a
pledge prevents a man of gentle breed-

ing from going to bed for the rest of his life?"

"Yes, madam," replied the Prince, "except with the lady to whom he is pledged."

"This is almost too strange to be true," observed the Fairy. "The poor boy must have been brought up in some utterly remote corner of the world. What a way to neglect a child's education!

"Really, my friend," she continued, "you must give me a better explanation than that, for even you yourself must feel that it is hardly satisfactory."

"Very well, then, madam," he replied, "since you order me to speak frankly to you, you must know that I have sworn an oath only to go to bed with virgins. An Oracle has decreed it."

"And for what do you take me, then,

pray?" asked the Fairy. "You seem to be taking a very great deal for granted."

"Madam," replied Zulmis, "I have been told that you are in the habit of going to bed with every one who has the honor of taking supper with you, and I presume that this is not the first day upon which you have ever had a guest at your table."

"That is true," she replied; "but there is nothing in that. I would sometimes, perhaps, even have preferred them to have forgotten themselves to the point of disrespect for me, instead of sleeping soundly all night long."

"What!" exclaimed the Prince. "Then all you want is that I should go to sleep beside you?"

"Of course," she replied. "I advise you to rearrange your ideas! I only want you to come to bed with me so that you may say how comfortable the bed is and speak well of my hospitality."

"Ah, madam!" said Zulmis, "under those conditions I willingly consent."

Whereupon he undressed, and the Fairy, in removing her shoes and stockings, gave the Prince a view, I don't know how, of two limbs, the sight of which was a real sedative to his senses.

At length, after a few courtesies as to who should get into bed first, they lay down beside one another; whereupon the Fairy said to him:

"By the way, I was forgetting to tell you before you went to sleep, that I am in the habit of dreaming and of telling stories in my dreams."

"I shall not mind at all, madam," replied the Prince, "provided you permit me not to listen to you."

Complete silence reigned between

them for a quarter of an hour. Then
from time to time Zulmis seemed to hear
the Fairy utter a word or two in a low
voice. He bent his attention, and this is
what he heard:

"A month ago a Prince came to bed
with me and was fool enough to let me
go to sleep; to punish him I changed him
into a badger."

On hearing this, poor Zulmis began to
tremble from head to foot; however, as
he had no desire to become a badger, he
began to edge nearer to the Fairy so as
to find how matters stood. But she suddenly made the following announce-
ment:

"A fortnight since, a Brahmin spent
the night by my side and had the insolence to try to seduce me; so I changed
him into a were-wolf."

With a bound Zulmis regained the

edge of the bed in time to avoid becoming a were-wolf, though he was very undecided as to whether the fate of a badger was a happier one.

The Fairy pretended to have been awakened by the sudden movement of the Prince.

"How is this?" she asked. "Are you not asleep yet?"

"Madam," he replied, stammering, "I was just about to drop off."

"Perhaps I disturbed your slumbers?" pursued the Fairy.

"Oh, not at all, madam!" he replied hastily.

"Have I not said anything yet?" she asked. "You must tell me if I do."

"Oh! You are too kind!" said the Prince, quaking with fear.

Silence fell again for half an hour. Zulmis was beginning to regain his calm, when the Fairy uttered these terrible words:

"If the Prince who is now by my side is awake, I am going to change him into a gray cat."

The Prince at once pretended to be asleep, and began to snore; but imagine his feelings when he heard the Fairy continue as follows:

"And if the same Prince is rude enough to be asleep, I shall change him into a poodle."

He immediately fell into a faint; the Fairy touched him and found him as cold as marble; by dint of attention and strong waters she revived him.

"What is the matter with you?" she asked him.

"Nothing, madam," he replied in a feeble voice.

"How, nothing?" insisted the Fairy.

"That is impossible: it is not your natural state."

"Pray forgive me for it, madam," he entreated.

"That is precisely what I cannot forgive you. You are as white as a ghost, and if you leave this house in such disorder, it will give me a bad name. In fact, in order to bring you back to your normal state, I am prepared to break the rule that I made for myself that I would always be indifferent to passion. You have moved me to compassion: draw nearer and I will make you happy."

This was exactly what Zulmis feared, but he nevertheless obeyed, and the Fairy clasped him to her; but Zulmis, suddenly moving his hand, touched something that felt like a shark's skin and, as he was already thoroughly frightened, he made a sudden bound.

Whereupon the Fairy seized her wand, touched him with it, and the unfortunate Zulmis became a very pretty little spaniel, and ran about the room barking loudly. The noise brought the women of the Palace hurrying in, and the Fairy had him chased out, although the weather was really not fit for a dog to be out in.

The Fairy laughed very heartily over this adventure; for it was the Fairy Mischief once more who had transformed herself in order to do Zulmis a service; as the sequel will show.

Zulmis, although very worried about his new shape, nevertheless accepted the situation like a good dog. He wondered whether to be forbidding or friendly, and came to the conclusion that it was better to be very gentle so long as he was only a stray dog, and that

he would never bark unless he happened
to become some lady's pet. He knew
that in that case the first duty of a small
dog is to yap when any one comes to pay
a visit. This gives his mistress an opening for making the prettiest speeches,
as, for instance, "What is the matter
with the little rascal, not knowing who
are our real friends?"

Zulmis, so that such might become his
fate, began to accustom himself in his
altered condition to dance between two
chairs, to jump through hoops and over
sticks, to beg, to mount guard, to walk
on three legs, and to bow every time any
one sneezed. But all these tricks tired
him very much, because his master was
always making him do them, so at last he
ran away, and after straying for eight
days and nights, he grew so weary of in-
sufficient food and of sleeping in the

open, that he resolved to attach himself
to the first person who would have him.
This happened to be a gardener return-
ing home after selling his vegetables in
the market. Zulmis went up to him,
fawned on him and followed him. The
gardener liked his looks, so, from that
moment, Zulmis became the gardener's
dog.

Those who know the necessary se-
quence of events in a story will hardly
be surprised to hear that this gardener
was the gardener of the Community of
Virgins of Isis.

Zulmis soon won the hearts of all his
new master's family. They thought him
so pretty and so graceful that they decided to make a gift of him to the Princess. Zulmis was anything but angry at
this turn of events, even though he did
not know who this Princess was: for he

felt certain that it would mean an improvement in his lot. He was to be given to her on the following day; he had already been accepted, and was being put through his tricks with great success; but what was his surprise when he recognized in the Princess his beloved Zelmaide. He kept on bowing, wriggling in the most astonishing way, barking delightedly and leaping up to Zelmaide, covering her with caresses, and wagging his tail like a dog who has found his lost mistress.

Zelmaide adored him and, indeed, for the first moment since the loss of her lover, her sadness seemed to weigh a little less upon her. She asked the little dog's name: no one knew it, so love suggested his real one, and she called him Zulmis. On being called by name, Zulmis redoubled his demonstrations and

made violent efforts to talk, but only succeeded in barking. The novelty of the
situation made the Princess shed a few
tears, which Zulmis hastened to lick
away.

"Alas!" sighed the love-lorn Zelmaide,
as she petted her little dog. "Alas, my
poor Zulmis! He whose name you bear
is a faithless lover who has deceived me
and forgotten me, and whom I still love."

This speech was interrupted by lamentations from Zulmis which touched
Zelmaide's heart.

"I see," she went on, "that you are
sorry for my woes. What heart, indeed,
could be so hard as not to be melted by
them, since even you are touched!"

Zulmis howled even louder at this, for
he was frantic with despair at being
forced to witness the sorrow and fidelity
of his mistress without being able to

open her eyes; he adored Zelmaide, and detested the Fairy I Don't Know What.

At this moment the Rose Queen entered her daughter's room. The first thing they talked about was the little dog; they said everything there was to be said about him, and then the Queen addressed the Princess as follows:

"Well, my dear daughter, what are you going to do? The Djinn knows the step you have taken, and, far from suspecting anything, he admires you and loves you more than ever, and begs to be allowed to see you."

"Ah, Mother!" replied Zelmaide, "I must admit my weakness to you. Zulmis still dominates my heart, though doubtless I shall never see him again; but I have abandoned myself to my fate: the thought of any other man is intolerable to me, and I would rather enroll

227

myself amongst the Virgins of Isis and devote my days to that goddess than betray Zulmis and impose upon the Djinn by accepting his hand."

At this the little dog began to howl again, and the Stolid Djinn walked in, accompanied by the Moderator.

On seeing his rival, Zulmis could not resist biting the fleshy part of his leg, which infuriated him and caused him to declare that dogs were forbidden in convents. But the Moderator interrupted him, saying:

"My lord, we allow the pupils to have them."

"And your Virgins?" insisted the Djinn.

"Oh! the Virgins? That is my business," replied the Moderator.

"Let us return to mine then," retorted the Djinn. "What is this I hear, Zelmaide? I am told that you are being childish, and wish to remain here. Of course I cannot prevent you from doing what you want, but really you do not know what you are giving up."

"I have a very shrewd idea," replied the Princess; "but my mind is made up."

"Really, madam," said the Stolid Djinn, addressing the Queen, "I never believed such virtue possible; I am losing something really fine to fall back, perhaps, on a pretty Princess who will play me some sorry trick. At all events that is always possible, and although I am by no means a fool—anyway I should not be the first; however, I am once more going to try to persuade Zelmaide," and he went on as follows: "Do you know, Princess, that when you join the Community of Virgins you can no longer have your dog with you?"

"I will give him to one of the pupils. Then I shall at least always be able to see him."

Zulmis immediately licked Zelmaide's hand: the Queen sneezed and he bowed; the Moderator dropped his handkerchief and he retrieved it; the Djinn tried to stroke him and he snarled at him.

"Yes," admitted the Djinn, "he is really a pretty dog. He can do everything but speak."

The visit lasted another hour without Zelmaide's resolution being shaken. It was even decided that she should take the veil in a month's time. This made a great stir in the Temple; the little dog continued to make an even greater stir. Each Virgin gave him comfits, biscuits, and jumbles, and he was the sole topic of conversation.

What things one sees when one is a

dog! I wish I could become one when I grow old!

Zulmis had succeeded so well in capturing the hearts of every one in the Temple, that each Virgin asked the Princess to let her have him for one day. Some of them even asked to be allowed to have him during the night. Zelmaide had not the heart to refuse. So that Zulmis sampled the beds of all the Virgins one after the other; and he was amazed to find that he always made a third!

In fact, Zulmis observed that all these young ladies always called themselves "Virgin" after their fifteenth birthday, in the same way that men often call themselves "Marquis." I do not know whether he communicated this discovery of his to the other dogs of the Temple, and that they have handed it down to the others; the fact remains that since that time no dog will do his tricks for fifteen-year-old maidens.

Zulmis recalled his dream, and realized that it had come true: his mistress had treated him like a dog, and he had gone to bed with all these beauties without being any the happier for it. And yet on the morrow Zelmaide was to take her vows. Zulmis determined to interrupt the ceremony, cost what it might. And so the sad moment arrived. The Virgins were all assembled in the Temple, surrounding the Queen, who sat in floods of tears to watch the sacrifice of her beloved Zelmaide. The sweet Princess was decked out like a victim, and was wearing her most lovely clothes only that she might strip herself of them a moment later, and plunge herself into eternal mourning. She shed a few tears as she left her room with her mother and her dear little dog, and said, in a voice broken with sobs and sighs:

"Mother, you bear witness to my fidelity. Zulmis! If only you knew that it is to you that I am immolating my-self!"

Little did she know what anguish her words caused him!

She arrived at the place appointed for her mournful vows. The Moderator was waiting, attired in his High Priest's robes, to receive her vows. Profound silence reigned in the Temple, and Zel-maide prepared to utter the fatal words. Her eyes were lowered, and her mother was holding a handkerchief to her own, when suddenly Zulmis leapt at the Mod-erator's face with such a nice judgment of distance that he tore his nose off with his teeth. The Moderator fell fainting

to the ground, and all the assembled
Virgins broke out into the most doleful
lamentations. Zelmaide remained mo-
tionless, and the Queen hid her laughter
in the handkerchief she had been using
for her tears. Angry hands seized Zulmis, and for a moment he was in peril
of his life; but the Queen rescued him,
promising to be responsible for him. In
the meantime the Chapter assembled,
and the Virgins unanimously con-
demned the Princess's dog to death, de-
claring that he must be handed over to
them and that they should be his judges.

The Princess was heartbroken, but
she did not dare say anything to oppose
this decree.

She was soon to plumb the very
depths of misery. At close of day, when
all the Virgins had retired, Zelmaide saw
the Fairy Mischief at her window in the

same chariot that had taken her to the Fairy Coquette. She felt that breeding demanded that she should ask politely after her health.

"Oh, Zelmaide! Zelmaide!" cried the Fairy. "I have come to tell you that an abominable crime is about to be committed, and that you can stop it."

"What is it?" asked the Princess.

"I know," replied the Fairy, "that you love Zulmis, but I want you to know that he adores you."

"Zulmis adores me?" cried the Princess. "Where is he now? Ah! Kind Fairy, take me to him in your chariot without delay."

"There is no need for that," she replied. "Your little dog, whom you call Zulmis, really is Zulmis: he is your lover, whom I changed into his present shape so that he should be able to be near you;

it is he who will be slain to-morrow before your eyes; he will only resume his human shape as he breathes his last, and his speech will only return to him to say to you, 'Zelmaide, I love you, and I die'."

The Princess burst into tears on hearing this, and nearly fainted. She did not faint only for fear of making matters worse.

"You can save his life," continued the Fairy, "by consenting to marry the Stolid Djinn."

"Alas!" lamented the Princess. "You know that it would be useless. Were I to accept the Stolid Djinn as my husband, he would want me to leave by the Gate of Ordeal. I should never get through it, and should merely get myself locked up here, without being able to save the life of Zulmis."

"Only give your consent," urged the Fairy. "I will arrange the rest."

"Can I trust you?" asked Zelmaide.

"Yes," answered the Fairy, "for now I am only serving you in order to annoy some one else."

With these words, which were far more reliable than her word of honor would have been, she disappeared. In the morning Zelmaide sent word to her mother that she had changed her mind and had decided to marry the Stolid Djinn immediately.

The Stolid Djinn, overwhelmed with joy, came to see her at once, and complimented her as follows:

"Well, so you have thought the matter over, have you? Faith! But you've acted wisely: I myself quite saw that in your heart you were dying to marry me, but dared not say so. See what it is to be timid. Your virtue really does delight me!"

He turned to the Priestess.

"Madam," he said to her, "I warn you that I shall marry the Princess tomorrow, that she is no longer yours, and that consequently her little dog is no longer under your authority; I pardon him and order him never to leave his mistress, for I don't care a fig whether your Moderator has a nose or not."

The Priestess was furious at this complete change of front, and Zulmis was in despair, imagining that the Princess had forgotten him, since she was marrying the Stolid Djinn; but that was only a dog's argument.

The Queen took the Djinn aside and said to him:

"My lord, I am sure you will not make my daughter leave by the Gate of Ordeal; it would prejudice her against you by giving her to understand that you doubted her virtue; and it would be doing her a great wrong, as the poor child is so simple and so innocent . . ."

"Allow me to inform you, madam," interrupted the Djinn, "that you do not know what you are saying, and if you were not Queen I should maintain that you were talking nonsense. Either your daughter has been a good girl or she has not; if she has, as I believe, she ought to be the first to ask to leave through the Gate of Ordeal; if, on the other hand—you understand me? Ah, then things will begin to happen! As she has never been anywhere but here, I will burn the house down, and the Moderator will not escape with the loss of his nose."

It was therefore decided that on the

following day the Stolid Djinn should lead Zelmaide out through the Gate of Ordeal in the presence of all the Virgins. The Queen did not sleep a wink all night, and the Princess was a little anxious herself, though she relied completely on the promise of the Fairy Mischief.

Never had there been a brighter day than the one destined to witness the Princess's marriage. The sun seemed to have put on a wedding garment, and was taking a delight in shedding more brilliance than usual, so as better to see how Zelmaide would face such an awkward situation.

The Djinn, magnificently instead of tastefully attired, came, accompanied by a numerous suite, to fetch the Princess, and led her towards the dangerous gate, which was so huge but which frequently became so small. All the Virgins were ranged on either side, and the Queen, carrying Zulmis in her arms, followed Zelmaide, being as solicitous as her daughter but much more fearful as to what would happen.

The Princess trembled: what had added to her fear was the sight beyond the gateway of an old and hideous Fairy who was known as the Fairy Janitress. The Stolid Djinn became aware of her reluctance, because he was beginning to have to drag her along, and so he began to harbor suspicions. But what was his surprise on seeing the portcullis fall and bar the way completely! The respect I have for a sex which I love prevents me from repeating the dreadful reproaches he made to Zelmaide. She was utterly confused and abashed, but suddenly the Fairy Janitress opened her dreadful

mouth and spoke the following reassuring words:

"My lord, mayhap 'tis you and not
Zelmaide that are the cause of what has
happened!"

"Oho! This is something quite new,"
sneered the Djinn. "Are you going to
suggest it is due to me that this Princess
is not all that she should be?"

"Not at all," answered the Fairy; "but
I think that 'tis you who are not all you
should be. Learn, then, the strange decree of the Djinn who cast a spell upon
this Gate. He ordained that it should
drop before damsels who no longer possess their pristine virtue; but he said further that it should also drop before men
who are still in possession of theirs.
Dare I ask your lordship if he is not in
that case?"

"Look at that dreadful woman," cried

the Stolid Djinn, "who thinks that before being married I have been capable of—'Sdeath, you are making me say stupid things!"

"Ah! you are the guilty one!" exclaimed the Fairy.

"'Zounds!" raged the Djinn; "do you call me guilty because I have always been good?"

The whole gathering, even the Princess, broke into laughter at this: which increased the Djinn's anger still more.

"There is but one way," said the Fairy Janitress, "of breaking this spell; that is to give me now what in any case you would not have retained for long."

"Give it to you, madam?" faltered the Djinn.

"Yes, my lord," she replied; "it is my perquisite."

"I should prefer," began the Djinn,

"to—But look at the dreadful hag: if I can only have the Princess at that price you may keep her: I repudiate her now and for all time."

Then the Fairy called the assembly to witness that the Stolid Djinn was incapable of marriage, and released the Princess from the obligation of marrying him.

"Oh, how pleased I am!" exclaimed the Princess.

"So-ho, my beauty!" cried the Djinn, almost breathless with rage, "you take it in that tone, do you? Very well, I will be revenged on you. I consent not to be your husband; but your fate is in my hands. I decree, therefore, that you shall not even be allowed to remain in this House, as I think there are too many consolations here."

"At least," said the Princess, "my little

dog will not leave me; you decided that yourself."

"That is true," he replied; "I regret it now, but I cannot withdraw it."

"But do you not see," asked the Fairy, "that you are losing all power over the Princess, if you deliver her to her lover?"

"Very likely; but what has that to do with it? Really, the woman is mad!" he said furiously.

At that instant the Fairy Janitress appeared in the form of the Fairy Mischief:

"Stolid and dull-witted Djinn!" she cried in a loud voice. "Behold your rival!"

And she touched the little dog with her wand; immediately he recovered the handsome figure of the Prince and threw himself at Zelmaide's feet, whilst the Djinn took himself off, wringing his hands and crying, "Oh, dear! Oh dear!"

The nuptials of the lovers were celebrated at once, and they say that Zelmaide was heard to cry out "Oh, dear!" too during the night, but in quite a different tone to that of the Djinn: which gives an air of probability to an old story which insists that Zulmis and Zelmaide lived happily together and had several children.

END OF "RHAPSODY RISQUE"

CPSIA information can be obtained at www.ICGtesting.com
Printed in the USA
BVOW06s1905140715

408793BV00014B/149/P